D1785592

MORE
JOY
THAN
PAIN

MORE
JOY
THAN
PAIN

Lars Rooth

Gracewing.

A Fowler Wright book produced in cooperation with the Vatican Radio

Originally published in Swedish by
Askelin & Hagglund, under the title
Det hande pa vagen, 2nd Ed. 1989

Gracewing Books are distributed

In Canada by   *In Australia by*
Novalis   Charles Paine Pty
PO Box 990   8 Ferris Street
Outremont H2V 457   North Parramatta
Canada   NSW 2151 Australia

First published by Fowler Wright Books 1991

All rights reserved. No part of this publication may be reproduced, stored
in a retrieval system, or transmitted in any form, or by any means,
electrical, mechanical, photocopying, recording or otherwise, without the
written permission of the copyright owner.

© Text 1991 Lars Rooth
Cc Original Swedish Edition
Lars Rooth 1988

ISBN 0 85244 190 8

Typesetting by Action Typesetting Limited, Gloucester
Printed and bound in Great Britain by Astec Press, Cardiff

Table of contents

v

Chapter 1

Background and Youth

In kindergarten, I proposed to a girl called Ingrid. I was considerate enough to warn her that she would be marrying a man with a dangerous profession — my ambition in those days was to join the fire brigade and stand atop a high ladder, exposed to all the perils.

I cannot remember if she accepted my proposal. She later married a minister in the Swedish Lutheran Church and became a mother of four. Her sister (ten years younger and not even born at that time) is now a Dominican nun and I myself a Jesuit priest. That could be something for statistical experts to ponder upon. My life does not fit into the mainstream of the law of averages, and I am rather grateful for it.

The kindergarten was located in the same apartment house in which I spent my first ten years. On present standards, Miss Barbro Ribbing would never have been permitted to use a small room in her parents' apartment for such purposes, and she probably did not have any formal qualifications for the job. She was somewhat of an ugly duckling in a family of tall and stately aristocrats, and I can imagine that she might have had certain problems of adjustment to the rest of the world. But not to us children, who loved her and really felt at home with her, whether we were busy with some little project in her room or out playing in the nearby parks and woods.

We belonged to the upper middle class and I suppose you could call us bourgeois. I can trace the family on my father's side back to the end of the 16th century, when they assumed the name of Rooth. Around 1800, one Carl Henric Rooth went to Helsingborg (across the water from Hamlet's Elsinore) and made it from errand boy to a proierous merchant. One of his sons was a successful merchant in Stockholm but went bankrupt during an economic crisis in the 1870's, and his son Otto, my grandfather, had to start earning money immediately after leaving school. He found employment as a travelling salesman and his district was the northern part of Sweden. In those days, covering the length of Sweden was anything but easy. The railway took him to Sundsvall (250 miles north of Stockholm), which geographically is the centre of the country. Here he changed to horse and sleigh, and some 400 miles and two weeks later, he reached his last stop, Haparanda, on the Finnish border. He stayed at the local inn and, judging by a photograph of the inn keeper, Mr Hertzman, it was a good place for eating and drinking; he almost looked like Humpty-Dumpty. His daughter Ellen became my paternal grandmother, and her playmate Eva married my maternal grandfather.

Eva's father owned a sawmill outside Haparanda and he used to travel to Paris every year to sell his wares. That entailed three weeks' journey by horse and sleigh to Gävle (550 miles), where the railway ended at that time and another week by train and ferries to reach Paris, where he would stay for one month before returning home in the same fashion. In other words, his yearly trip to Paris took three months, which to us seems rather like an extended vacation. Travelling at that pace was undoubtedly a good way to avoid stress.

My maternal grandfather took his engineer's degree in Gothenburg and found work at a sawmill in Luleè, near the northern tip of the Baltic. Soon, the family moved to Kiruna, the new iron ore centre north of the polar circle, where my grandfather became chief assistant to the head of the project, Hjalmar Lundbom, a fellow student from the school of engineering. Kiruna was virgin ground and grandfather, who did much of the town planning, became the first chairman of the local council.

Lundbom remaining unmarried, my grandmother acted as hostess at the official company celebrations. She was a very able person with a strong feeling for social justice. She noticed that the local merchants treated the Lapps in an unfair way, accepting their goods — mainly game and hides — in exchange for coffee, sugar, salt and other necessities.

It turned out that the Lapps were always in the red, however much they brought in. So my grandmother paid the nomads cash for their goods and then sold it to the merchants at the same price.

My mother, born in Luleè but brought up in Kiruna, was the eldest of four daughters. Three of them became teachers of physical education, getting their diplomas at an institute in Lund in the very south of Sweden. My mother was a good gymnast and was included in the Swedish troup performing at the Olympic Games in Stockholm in 1912. Had women been allowed to compete in fencing at that time, she would probably have made the fencing team, also. I was very proud of her when, at the age of around 40, she won the first form of downhill race for women, held in Åre. My paternal grandfather engaged in business of various kinds and had his ups and downs, without ever hitting rock bottom. He was one of the founders of what is now the Swedish State Lottery and it is as its first head that I remember him — a bit awe-inspiring and not very communicative. My grandmother, on the other hand, was one of the most charming and kind persons I have ever known, and their home was open to every one. Many people in need found their way to her and grandfather supported her charity generously.

My father Ivar was the eldest of four children. After having studied law in Uppsala and economics in Berlin, he was to spend all his life in banking. In my youth, he was assistant director of Inteckningsbanken in Stockholm where Ivar Kreuger, the financial wizard of the period, was a member of the board, participating actively in the daily operations of the bank. At the age of 40, my father was made governor of the Bank of Sweden, partly due to his active membership in the Liberal Party. From then on he abandoned politics in order to be a civil servant, above party lines. His tasks turned out to be more difficult than expected. The stock market crashed in New York soon after his appointment, in 1931 he had to recommend that Sweden leave the gold standard. In 1932, the financial empire of Kreuger fell apart and my father had to take his former superior to task. In a letter, the Bank of Sweden urged Kreuger to explain his complicated loans. He reacted by taking his life. My father was anything but a tough business man, but he never had any qualms of conscience about his role in the Kreuger affair.

As governor of the Bank of Sweden, he laid great stress on international relations and travelled abroad regularly. He formed personal friendships with many leading bankers in Europe and was held in great esteem by them, probably more so than at home — he was left stranded in 1948, after resigning from his post at the Bank of Sweden due to disagreement on fiscal policy. In 1951, having worked on a project in Iraq for the World Bank, he was elected managing director of the International Monetary Fund in Washington (which in those days was less agressive in its policies). Two years later, Dag Hammarskjöld was elected secretary general of the United Nations and the two again met regularly. In the early thirties, Dag had been recommended to my father as a promising young man and Dag became his personal assistant. I remember him turning up for Sunday breakfast with a shorthand pad in the pocket. He soon advanced, however, and it was not long before he became president of the board of directors of the Bank of Sweden. He and my father held similar views on the value of dedicated public service coupled with involvement in international affairs, and they remained close friends.

* * *

My first earliest recollections take me back to our summer holidays at Dalarö in the Stockholm archipelago. Little incidents left traces in the memory of the three-year-old boy: a glass veranda, the rowboat in which we crossed to visit a ship builder, falling into the water but being rescued immediately by my mother.

The outing to the main square. My sister Elsa, 9, and my brother Gösta, 6, were away for the day and I had been left at home with Märtha, our nurse. I sat in a small sailing boat built up on land when along came the neighbour's boy Anders Franzén (later renowned for finding the 17th century man-of-war "Wasa", now on exhibit in Stockholm).

—Where are you off to? I asked.

—The main square, to buy a paper.

—Can I can come with you?.

—Are you allowed to? he asked, somewhat sceptically, but I told him "sure" and off we went. With my short legs, the distance seemed rather long and there were many things to look at and admire, and a long time passed before I returned home. Märtha, who had not been informed of my absence, was quite upset, being convinced that I must have fallen into the sea. So I got a hiding, which was well deserved. However, it was the only time that she laid hands on me and later she felt sorry that this incident should be one of my earliest memories.

Physical punishment, by the way, was a rare thing in our family. My sister, (like my mother and grandmother before her, I am told) just got more stubborn if punished, whereas my brother would be upset even by harsh words and afterwards had to be consoled. As for myself, I did not react much when admonished slightly, but a real reprimand would make me docile as a lamb.

* * *

After kindergarten, I attended a private elementary school. Sitting still in class was a problem. Across the road, there was a Lutheran church, where we once gathered for some special commemoration. I got bored waiting for the ceremony and started some mischief, whereupon I was moved and had to sit between the head mistress and the games mistress. (Years later, I found out that the latter had become a Catholic, and she was pleased to find one of her pupils studying for the priesthood. However, she died before my ordination.)

I liked our teacher very much, which made a lot of difference to me. Right through school, I would do well if I got on with the teacher, but tended to neglect the subject if I did not care for them.

The way to and from school was interesting and we thought up all sorts of exciting games, like looking for escape ways if any one were to chase us. We found a perfect one at Birgerjarlsgatan 36. Up the stairs, a flight and a half, cut across a yard and out we came on a different street. Perfect, except for one thing. We had to ring the bell and wait for the caretaker to open, which he did by pressing a release in his flat on the first floor. Then you had to wait downstairs until he gave up checking who it was, or nip up quickly before he started looking. One day, I missed my timing and a huge man took me by the scruff of my neck and carried me into the street. I was so frightened that I wet my pants, a memory which came back in a flash when I some 45 years later visited the same building to inquire about a rest home for my mother.

After four years, I was sent to a secondary school in Stockholm, but I never cared much for it. Our form master during all those eight years was a good teacher but, unfortunately, had what would to-day be called gay tendencies. I do not say that as an accusation, because he certainly did not molest us, but we could not help but notice his attitudes and his changing favouritism, which made us feel uneasy, without really understanding why.

Things might have been easier if we had been given some kind of education about sex, but that did not exist in my days. When I got my first information on the subject from a class mate — at a rather tender age — I asked mother about it, but she did not manage even to start answering my question. When my father, much later, tried to talk to me about the subject, he restricted himself to warning me of the dangers of loose women and venereal disease.

* * *

I wanted to spend the last four years in another school in order to learn Latin and Greek, which was not taught in our school. My mother discussed the matter with the rector, who was usually kind and helpful. But no, he saw not reason for my not staying on. After all, he said, Lars has done well in mathematics, and his brother is a pupil here as was his father and uncle. That was it, unfortunately, without further discussion. I have learnt Latin later on in life, but I did not particularly enjoy my last years at school.

Life was not just school, however. At an early age, I was sent to dancing classes and afterwards, we formed a group that met every other Saturday and we kept it going for years. Arrangements were very simple; we met at the home of one of the group, each family taking their turn. Music was provided for by records, played on a portable grammophone, wound by hand. In the interval, tea and sandwiches were served, but no one was allowed to offer extras as it could have started a competition. If the apartment was big enough, the parents would retire to another room and play bridge. We preferred to be left on our own most of the time. That did not lead to any excesses, however.

Alcoholic drinks were hardly ever provided, except for a glass of wine on special occasions, and we had not even heard of drugs, thank heavens. We had our romantic attachments, but did not indulge in sex, apart from an occasional kiss and some hugging in a corner of a sofa. On Sundays, we would go for walks or ski. In spite of the fact that we came from reasonably well off families, we did not have much pocket money. We took in a film or a concert occasionally, but never went out to a restaurant to eat. It all seems rather simple and innocent in retrospect, but we enjoyed ourselves and did not feel frustrated or hemmed in.

* * *

Now there is one thing I have not dealt with in this chapter and that is the fact that when I was eight, my parents separated and subsequently my mother and I lived on our own. This was such a big thing to get adjusted to that I prefer to leave it to a later chapter, in which I try to sort out the reasons for becoming a Catholic.

Chapter 2

To Become an Actor...

The ambition to join the fire brigade soon faded and another one took its place: to became an actor. It lasted many a year. As children, we tried our hand at setting up our own little plays during summer vacations, but soon we had the chance to see real theatre in action. I remember a delightful performance of The Merry Widow, staged in the Concert Hall of Stockholm in 1931 with Gösta Ekman, a famous actor, and Zarah Leander — what a show! Ekman, in evening dress and white gloves, entered the stage by a revolving door, took three rounds through it before stepping out onto the stage, and the audience loved it.

A theatre in Stockholm called Oscar's often staged operettas, which went down well in our family. You can imagine my eagerness when one day our music teacher asked a couple of boys to stay on after class for an audition, as the management at Oscar's was looking for some one to sing the role of the Dauphin in The Three Musketeers. I did not have much of a voice but that did not stop me from asking the teacher if I could not also be given a chance. He let me sing a few bars and decided that it was all right for me to go along, if I wanted to.

And did I! As soon as school ended, I rushed to the theatre and asked for Håkan von Eichwald, the musical director, who was in charge of selecting candidates for the cast. I can't remember what I sang, nor do I recollect what von Eichwald said, but shortly after an overjoyed boy arrived home to tell his mother that he had got an engagement at Oscar's. Having tried to reason with me, without success, she called the bank and enlisted dad's help. He called von Eichwald saying that he took it for granted that my lack of talent for singing

8

had already decided the matter. If that was not the case, however, he just wanted to inform Mr Eichwald that under no circumstances would his son be allowed to start playing every evening at a theatre. That was it. A promising career had come to a halt, even before starting. It is extraordinary how obtuse parents can be at times. They tried to tell me that it was impossible to combine school and working at a theatre. But if other boys could, why not I? To make up for things, dad later took me to see a performace of The Three Musketeers, but that almost made it worse, because the boy who took the part of the Dauphin did not have to sing a single note. There blew one of their main arguments.

If I could not perform myself, however, at least I could see other people doing it. Luck had it that Hans, a classmate of mine, was the son of Alice and Ernst Eklund, a famous pair of actors, who also ran a small theatre. Thus I was able to see many performances from their private box — I especially remember The Begger's Opera. It was a privilege to get to know Alice and Ernst Eklund. There was a striking contrast between seeing them in action and privately. As soon as they appeared on the stage, they dominated it, whereas at home they were unpretentious to the point of appearing to be shy. I could hardly believe they were the same people.

The Royal Dramatic Theatre offered inexpensive matinées and special performances for school children, which gave us city dwellers the chance of seeing a lot of theatre at little expense. My favourite actress was Inga Tidblad. Her interpretation of roles like Rosalind in As You Like It was not only delightful to watch but you could sense how she enjoyed playing these Shakespearean comedies. There was also a memorable performance of Steinbeck's Of Mice and Men with Lars Hansson and Holger Löwenadler. People were so taken by it that even during the interval they hardly uttered a word.

I remember too Signe Hasso. Her Ophelia was almost translucent. She soon left for the States and I met her a few times when I lived in New York City 1941 – 43, and that gave me a chance to admire her not only from afar. By the way, New York is a wonderful place if you like the theatre. There I saw Alfred Lunt and Lynn Fontaine performing together, and Tallulah Bankhead in Thornton Wilder's The Skin of

Our Teeth — a tour de force which was not bettered by Vivien Leigh, whom I later saw in London in the same role. And then Basil Rathbone in Arsenic and Old Lace, that ever popular play. I saw it again several years later, while studying theology near Oxford, where it was performed by my co-seminarians. I found that their version could well stand up to being compared with the New York one. Jesuits do have a long tradition of staging plays.

The first time I was to perform in public was at school, where the literary society asked me to play the role of Lotta, a girl. It never came off, actually, but to my annoyance, some of my classmates called me Lotta for a long time afterwards.

My real début came in England, where we put on plays during garden parties. It was at a small school near Bournemouth, where I was given a part in a French play, together with a Polish and an Italian boy. At one point, I completely forgot my line. However, I made a grand gesture and said — in German! — to my opposite number: "You just carry on and I'll be right with you." Having heard his next line, I was indeed back in again and nobody the wiser for it all.

Now that is a lesson that I had use for later in life. Even in liturgy, things can go wrong. The important thing is to carry on with dignity. I was once asked to officiate at a wedding ceremony between a young German and a Swedish girl in the old church of Östersund, up in the northern provinces of Sweden. After an initial hymn, I read the Gospel and preached, whereupon a lady sang something appropriate. The next point on the program was the blessing of the rings, but they were still in the sacristy, and I did not have a server to send for them. The only solution left was to fetch them myself in a solemn one-man procession. It worked out beautifully and I arrived back just as the last bars of the song faded out. I put the silver platter on the altar, turned around and told the people that now I was going to bless the rings.

Afterwards, a lady came up to me and declared that being a Protestant, this was the very first time that she had attended a Catholic service. Some of the ceremonies are rather similar to ours, she said, some of them not. But

the thing that had made the greatest impression on her was
the blessing of the rings...

* * *

Does that mean that as a priest, I have found a certain
outlet for my ambitions to be an actor? Well, I certainly
hope that I have not been just playing to the gallery. I doubt
that I would have dared to become a minister in the Swedish
Lutheran Church, where so much emphasis is placed on the
sermon, giving it almost sacramental dimensions. I would
feel almost embarrassed trying to lift my own words to such
a lofty level.

In an interview in Svenska Dagbladet on Dec. 30, 1987,
the Swedish actress Lena Granhagen stated that "you can
compare the stage to the womb — both are empty, holy
spaces...To actors, the stage must be a holy place."

In the Catholic liturgy, celebration of the sacrifice of the
Mass is the centre of a divine drama, where bread and wine
are living symbols, portraying Christ, yes, even making him
present among us. The priest is a servant in the temple,
who takes on the role of Christ when pronouncing the
words of consecration, in the same way that Christ did at
the Last Supper. He does it in persona Christi — on his
behalf and in his stead. Consequently, he is no longer just
portraying a role; human limits have been transcended and
it becomes a Sacrament, "the regal way of Christianity to the
ultimate experience of reality", as the Norwegian Dominican
Fr Hallvard Rieber-Mohn once put it. Here man is able to
grip on the very hem of God's own robe, and divine power
starts flowing into his human existence, giving it life and
renewing it.

A Catholic priest shall indeed also preach the Word of
God, but that is not all that he does. One day, after Mass,
a member of the congregation told me rather bluntly: "Well,
you were not very inspired to-day, Father, were you?" —
"No", I replied, "but you can't be inspired every time."

And I thank Heaven for the fact that the Mass does not
stand and fall with my sermon.

* * *

After this theological excursion, I would like to tell you
about the peak of my theatrical career. It was actually off
stage and without any public. It was Christmas 1939, and I

was spending the holidays at a skiing resort in Sweden. One day, I found myself in a corner of the entrance hall, reading a book printed on India paper. In came Viveca Lindfors, quite ravishing as usual. She was at that time studying at the Royal School of Drama in Stockholm. (Not long afterwards, she became well-known as an actress both in Sweden and the United States, but I am afraid that her success was greater on the stage than in private life).

"What are you reading", she asked. " The Bible?"

"Heavens no", I replied, "this is Shakespeare."

I had a lovely edition of his complete works, bought at Selfridge's in London for only 5 shillings. It turned out that she had never read him in the original. "A crying shame", I said, and decreed that it had to be put right immediately.

So we repaired to my lodgings, where we slept in bunk beds, as in a night train. I knew the whole of the balcony scene from Romeo and Juliet by heart, so I let her climb up onto the top bed, with the book in her hand, while I stayed down below. And thus, I was the first person to play Romeo to her Juliet.

Chapter 3

Summers at Home and in Germany

When I was four, we left the summer abode at Dalarö and moved to Kaanan on Lake Mälaren. To-day, it is a public beach, the whole region having changed character and become part of the suburbs of Stockholm. The house we lived in at Kaanan is still there. When I visited it some years ago, it was used as a coffee shop and in what had been dad's bedroom, there was a big juke box – not really his style.

Some memories linger from those days: the pink guest room in the loft, where my maternal grandmother lived, with me sitting at the end of her bed, early in the morning, trying to count to 100. The pig that was slaughtered and the messy preparation of black-pudding. The farmer's old horse, which we led to the far end of the enclosure where we climbed up to ride on her. She did not like it much, and returning to the exit gate, she would choose a path where the branches hung low and hoped that they would brush us off.

The reef where we went fishing. When dad went to check the net he took me along. I was sitting in the bow of the small dinghy when we heard my brother calling for help. Dad rowed so fast that water splashed over the sides on to me, and after pulling the dinghy up temporarily on the ncarcst shore, he ran off to find out what was happening. My cousin Bengt had fallen from the jetty into the water and had been caught so unfortunately in the structure that he drowned. As this was my first encounter with death, it was rather beyond my comprehension.

I was really more frightened by the snake. Most of the path to the outhouse was shaded by bushes, but just before reaching it, there was an open spot, and there a snake was

basking in the sun. I put my bare foot right across it, and I
can still feel it wriggling from under my foot. Fortunately, it
was not of a poisonous species, but that made no difference
to me. I shut myself into the outhouse and screamed until
some one came to my rescue. The phobia about snakes has
never left me, and to this very day, I recoil from them, even
when seeing them on a TV screen.

* * *

In the early 1930's, our summer routine was changed, as
my parents separated and my father remarried (something
I will return to later). We children were to divide our holidays between the two homes. During the winter season,
we usually went skiing with mother up in the mountain
regions of Sweden. Four summers in a row, mother rented
a place near Båstad (well-known for its tennis tournaments),
a wonderful place for young boys, with lots of new friends,
tennis, swimming and horse-back riding.

My father moved to a new place in the southern archipelago of Stockholm where we did a lot of sailing, first
with the larger boat belonging to my father, then with a
smaller one given to us two boys after dad sold his. Sailing
in the Baltic was considerably more interesting than on Lake
Mälaren.

In the summer of 1935, I spent three weeks at a sailing
school near Karlskrona in southern Sweden (later famous for
the Russian submarine on the rocks). I enjoyed those weeks,
but they were tough. We had to climb the masts of old sailing
ships — not an easy task, as I suffer badly from vertigo. We
sailed in small boats, pulled the oars of heavy navy life boats
and made day trips with medium size sailing boats. One of
the latter had as captain Ebbe Lieberath Jr, the son of the
founder of the Swedish branch of the boy scouts. After
returning home from school in the afternoon, I had often
listened to his father on the radio, telling stories about small
boys volunteering to help poor frail women by fetching water
and wood for them, and the stories always ended with the
same phrase: "And that was, of course, a boy scout." I did
not particularly take to that type of sturdy ethical injunctions
and promised myself never to become a boy scout. I had the
feeling that Ebbe Jr felt rather the same way.

We then went on a two-week trip on a schooner of 125

tons with a crew of some 30 boys. It was a great experience standing at the wheel of a ship that size, but I am afraid that the officers were not quite up to scratch. We spent a couple of days tacking against heavy winds to get from Bornholm to Copenhagen and lost the motor lifeboat just because it had not been picked up on deck in time. Due to the high wind, the main sail had to be taken in and later one of the foresails was badly torn in the wind. After that, we had to sail with the wind and get into a port in Sweden for repairs. Those of us who did not get sea sick had to be available for manoeuvres at all hours. So I disembarked in Gothenburg quite exhausted. Having served me a good meal, my mother and a friend of hers started making the bed, while I got into my pyjamas. Before they had finished, I was in bed and sound asleep. I did not wake up for 18 hours.

* * *

From Gothenburg, mother and I went to the island of Rügen in northern Germany. It was my second trip abroad. The first one, in 1929, had taken us via Copenhagen to Föhr, one of the northern Friesan islands, and back via Hamburg. Much had happened between 1929 and 1935. I had grown and was able to observe my surroundings. Hitler had assumed power in 1933, and though it had not yet made that much difference in Thiessow, the small seaside resort where we stayed, it was here that I got my first impressions of Nazi mentality. Right in the middle of the promenade, which was milling with people, I heard a young boy half singing, half shouting: Ein Jude hier, ein Jude hier, hier sollte man ein Messer haben — there is a Jew around, I wish I had a knife. No one, but no one uttered a word of protest or even comment. From that day on, I never had any illusions about the Third Reich. And I am sure that if I had had any, my father would have made a point of putting me right.

The next summer found me in Germany again. Getting a good working knowledge of languages was an important part of our education. A banker friend in Hamburg, Erich Warburg, found a family near Magdeburg who were interested in an exchange. They lived in a castle with 71 rooms, several of them large ceremonial halls, with a moat around it and some 7,500 acres of farmland and forest. In the morning, Otto, the butler, would wake me early with a cheerful Morgenstund hat Gold im Mund (the German version of the early bird catching the worm), and leave a can of hot water for me. I was supposed to get up and participate in the 7 o'clock morning prayers which the lady of the house conducted for the servants — and those members of the family and guests who got up in time. I am afraid that the water in the can was usually tepid before I reached for it.

On my arrival, Otto seemed quite relieved to learn that I was a Lutheran — "we all are, in these parts", he said. The family had three children; a girl, a boy who was a few years younger than me, and an even younger boy who was rather spoilt. Being the oldest one, I was expected to set a good example to the others, which I did not particularly enjoy. The father of the house was very kind and I often travelled around the estate with him in horse-drawn buggy. I vividly remember the endless rows of beet sugar plants, and tenant families on their knees along them, tending them in the scorching sun. Maybe that is the reason why I regularly thank the Lord that he did not make me a farmer.

Instead of attending the village school, the children at the castle were instructed by a governess, who was a thoroughly convinced Nazi. When I asked her for some extra reading matter, she brought along a whole stack of the SS weekly Der Stürmer, a publication whose very text and illustrations made me physically sick. At the same time, the governess wanted to affect good manners. One day, when she came into the class room, a strong smell of manure poured in through the open window. So she turned to me and said: "Lars, please close the window. Es riecht nach Fisch — there is a smell of fish", which immediately became our favourite comment in all sorts of situations.

In a sermon, the local pastor had ventured to criticise the persecution of the Jews, for which he was sentenced to three months in jail. "And quite right, too", was the comment of the lady of the castle. "We should not presume to set ourselves up against those who have been given authority over us". Although the children did not attend the village school, the boy was a member of the Hitlerjugend and the girl of the parallel organisation Bund deutscher Mädel. I was invited to participate in their games where we competed in a 100 meter dash, the long jump and throwing, but the object

thrown was not a ball but a wooden thing in the shape of a
skittle. It did not enter my mind at the time that we were
training to throw something that was just the size of the
German hand grenade. I managed to qualify for the medal
called Siegesnadel (victory medal). It was presented in the
village square and I instinctively refrained from joining the
rest of the youth as they marched in their uniforms through
the village.

After a while, we left for Stolpmünde, a Baltic seaside
resort near the so-called Polish corridor. We were joined by
a young family, Baron and Baroness von Knigge with two
small children, relatives of the family I was staying with and
friends of Erich Warburg's. They had been instrumental in
arranging the exchange which made my stay possible. Erich
Warburg, by the way, being a member of a Jewish family,
would have been rather upset if he had known the influence
of Nazi ideas in my surroundings. Knigge was a well-known
name in Germany as an earlier Baron Knigge had written the
standard book on etiquette. I remember our young Knigge
family as an excellent example of good manners and their
kindness made my stay much easier.

One day we visited the home of nobles who were relatives
of the family I was staying with. They had an estate of 70,000
acres, a castle with a lovely marble staircase and something
that made a great impression on me: in the centre of the
large dining room table stood a big circular contraption,
laden with all sorts of delicacies. It was mounted on ball
bearings. With just a slight touch of the hand, you could
set it in motion until your favourite dish appeared right in
front of you.

It was the summer of Hitler's Berlin Olympic Games. At
home, we were very much interested in sports, so I rented a
small radio and spent a lot of time listening to reports from
the games, which did not make me very popular with my
host family. On the return journey, I left them in Berlin,
where a Norwegian friend took me to the actual Olympic
games — a land hockey match between India and Japan,
and some swimming. Not the most important events, but it
was exciting to be there in person, all the same.

The following year, we received our exchange guest, but it
was not one of the children of the family but Rosemarie, a

poor relative who lived at the castle. She was around 20 and had looked after me when I happened to feel misunderstood or unjustly treated, and had thus become somewhat of a favourite of mine. I was so taken by the news that she was to spend a month with us that I lost my appetite, and my mother got rather worried. Being 15 years old, I could hardly tell her that I was head over heels in love with Rosemarie. However, I did manage to discuss the matter with the girls in the dancing group and that helped me to put it into perspective. When Rosemarie arrived, I was overjoyed and we talked, looked at all the interesting things in Stockholm, and I can remember us going to see the film Lost Horizon, with me translating for her. There was undoubtedly somewhat of a Shangri-La atmosphere over those days, as far as I was concerned. However, when she left, that was it, and I returned to normal life and more suitable romantic attachments to girls in the dancing group.

*   *   *

An epilogue. When the Russians were about to take over the German districts east of the Elbe river, Erich Warburg, by now a colonel in the U.S.Army, went to the castle near Magdeburg to fetch the family and take them to their relatives in the British zone of occupation. The father of the family took defeat and the loss of the family property so hard that he suffered a stroke and died.

Many years later, I was in Göttingen, helping out in the Jesuit parish. This was not far from where Rosemarie's own family lived, and I visited them to find out whether she was at home. However, she had married and moved away. As my host family lived close by, I visited them instead. Frau von X. was there, and she expressed surprise and regret that we had not sent them food packages after the war − "after all, we were so nice to you". "And what about the Nazis?" I ventured to ask. "Oh, we were always against them!"

I cannot help feeling that it is not all that unreasonable that the great estates were confiscated and turned into collective farms instead. That was an almost inevitable development under the circumstances.

Chapter 4

Two Summers in England

When I attended school, we had eight years of German, six of English and five of French. It was therefore natural to dedicate my summers to developing the three languages in that order. Now the time had come for English, and I was glad to be able to travel westwards, after having lived in a Germany where Nazism was getting stronger all the time, something we noticed even in Sweden. Several of our Jewish friends were spending increasingly large sums of money to help their relatives to leave Hitler's domains.

Consequently, my expectations were high when in June 1937 I left for England to spend a large portion of the summer at a small school near Bournemouth. It might sound a bit strange to go to school during summer holidays, but it was actually a very good idea. With few exceptions, the other boys spoke English as their mother tongue, and I took all sorts of subjects, which helped me to get an all-round vocabulary. As a temporary pupil, there was no need to strain myself to get more than average marks.

Cranemoor, at Hinton Admiral railway station, near the border of the New Forest, was a small private school, run by the rector/owner without great ambitions, and with a small number of teachers at his disposal. The school catered especially for boys from the colonies, whose parents were on long sabbatical home leaves. There were for instance the bright and lively Krikler brothers from Bulawayo in what was then Southern Rhodesia. Others were there because of some handicap, which made it difficult for them to attend other schools. Thus my friend Peter Walker had a bad limp, whereas John L., a close relative of the royal family, suffered from mental retardation. He could immediately tell you on

19

what day of the week the 14th of July 1789 fell, but when we had to write an essay on the subject "What would I do if I had £100,000", he had only managed to spend 17/6 s. at the end of the period. Only three of us, myself, an Italian and a Polish boy did not have English as our mother tongue, but even that had its advantages. We were better at spelling, having picked up our knowledge of English out of books and not by ear.

When the summer term ended, I was invited to stay a couple of weeks with Peter Walker, whose family lived in Lymm, Cheshire. We strolled around the fields, shot rabbits, and went to visit Manchester, which at that time was much dirtier than to-day. I found a mackintosh raincoat at a factory sale and wearing it, I thought that I looked like a real Englishman.

It was with great pleasure that I returned to England the following summer, this time to another school called Bedales, near Petersfield, Hampshire. It has since become quite well-known as Princess Margaret sent her children there. In 1938, its reputation stemmed more from the fact that it was a co-educational boarding school, something very unusual at that time. It catered for another type of clientèle than Cranemoor. I was surprised to find out that some of the girls had ample clothing accounts, in spite of the fact that their daily apparel was the school uniform.

The number of pupils per class was small and we found it easy to get on with the teachers. Their attitude was to encourage, rather than force us to learn. Instead of just giving grades in the end-of-term report, they would write some personal comments like: "Showed interest and made good progress in a short time". Now, being in England, the subject mentioned first on the report was sports. I had made the school swimming team for the breast stroke, not because I was much good at it, but because hardly any one else seemed to know how to do it. History was quite interesting, dealing with the colonial period, of which I knew very little, and the teaching was very relevant as the British Empire was still intact in the 1930's.

Education at Bedales was somewhat influenced by anthroposophical ideas. This was most noticeable in gymnastics, which was conducted with the help of music and smooth body movements — quite different from the sturdy exercises I had been subjected to in Sweden under the auspices of a former army officer. Music was held in high esteem at Bedales, and I remember pupils as excellent soloists in Mozart's oboe quartett and a Haydn cello concerto. Even the general standard was high. In chapel we formed ourselves into four groups — sopranos, altos, tenors and basses, and every one was trained to sing their part straight from the music.

There was one thing about chapel that I found somewhat perplexing. The teachers took turns to plan morning prayers during the week and they had a free hand. For a whole week, we listened to a girl reading from Alice Through the Looking-Glass. I like Lewis Carroll as an author, but I still have not managed to work out how he came under the subject of morning prayers.

I enjoyed my time at Bedales, with one exception. We slept in dormitories and I was together with six or seven other boys of various ages. There I encountered not only bullying but roughness with clear sexual overtones of a type I was not used to. With a male unmarried housemaster, there tended to be a somewhat one-sided atmosphere as far as sex was concerned.

I must confess that I am doubtful about the advisability of placing boys at an early age in boarding schools, making them spend years, including those of puberty, away from normal family life and surroundings. My hesitation stems not only from the risk of one-sided sexual development (which was less of a risk at Bedales). My reasons are more basic and simple: What does a small boy do if he is feeling homesick or has other personal problems? Where does he find arms to embrace him and give him a feeling of security, or a chance to cry in his misery? It seems to me that the traditional English stiff upper lip may hide quite a few complexes, which could have been avoided through a more natural and humane form of education.

After Bedales, I was again invited to stay with Peter Walker in Cheshire. His parents took us on various excursions, this time to North Wales, a part of Britain that I was to get to know more intimately during a training period in the British Army.

On the way back to Sweden, I travelled in the company of Per Holmgren, whose father, the pastor of the Swedish Lutheran parish in London, had been transferred to Stockholm. We stood together in the stern of the ship as it steamed out through the Thames estuary and we both felt that we were going the wrong way. After all, what was small little Sweden, compared to England? Wasn't everything in Great Britain much more wonderful? We already longed to return.

It took me years of living abroad before I changed my opinion on this subject. That does not mean that I now believe that Sweden is better than other countries, but I have learnt the great importance of having "roots". They are part of your personality and transplanting them into a foreign soil is a much more complicated and delicate operation than to change a mere passport.

Chapter 3

Europe on the Eve of War

My father was on one of his trips abroad when I finished
secondary school in 1939, but he had left a letter to be read
out. In it he recalls having to complain quite often that I
"did not work as hard at school as I should have". That was
quite true, but then my outlook on life was rather different
than that of my father's. My idea at school was to avoid
having poor marks at the end of the scholastic year, because
then you had to pay for it by studying during the summer
holidays. My first teacher of physics was an old man, who
remembered having taught my father — and dubbed him "a
model pupil". I was practically in tears over it; to my mind,
it was about the worst thing one could say about a person.
But my father was of the same generation as King Gustav
VI Adolf of Sweden, whose motto was "Duty above all",
an ideal which I do not share. It sounds too much like Kant's
categorical imperative. I am by no means unwilling to do my
share of work, but I have to be motivated for it. Maybe my
results at school would had been better if they had let me
study classics instead. The three last terms, however, I was
more diligent, as I wanted to qualify for a commercial college
in Stockholm which was rather selective.

We took our written exams in March, and if you passed
them with above average results, the later oral exam was
merely a question of formality. I did reasonably well, except
in Swedish composition — my paper was badly written, both
as far as content and form were concerned. Forty years later,
at a class reunion, some one brought up the fact that the two
of us who were professionally engaged in writing had both
got poor marks in the final test in Swedish composition.
Passing out of school was a big event in those days —

23

we felt as if we had been given a key to the future (and consequently, failing was a disaster). Relatives and friends were waiting outside to see us coming out, wearing the white student's cap. Bedecked with flowers, we were hoisted in the air. We competed to devise unusual ways to be transported home and I managed a "first": our school was next-door to the tram terminal, so I ordered my own personal tram. It stopped for me right in front of the school. They even had it decorated with greenery and we went on a trip through town in style, singing and cheering. The company must have charged it to their publicity account, because we paid practically nothing for it.

During the following weeks, we led the most care-free existence you could imagine. Every day, we went to a different school to cheer the arrival of another lot of students, fresh out of school. With my brand new student's cap, I had free entry to any reception held at their homes, and quite frequently, I was invited to a dinner-dance in the evening to celebrate a fellow student. The parties were still held in private homes, not at a restaurant. Food was more lavish, but apart from some wine, alcoholic drinks were seldom served (I remember only one instance where some of those present had a few too many).

The spring that year was really beautiful. After the party, we went for a walk on one of the many islands on which Stockholm is built or climbed the heights above the estuary of the Baltic sea to watch the sun rise (which it does around three o'clock a.m. in the month of May). For the first time in my life, I became aware of the beauty of my home town. Other cities may be more renowned for their architectural gracefulness, but few fit as perfectly into their natural geographical settings as Stockholm does.

We did not let the text of the students' song about a bright, promising future fool us too much — after all, the year was 1939, with the threat of war ever increasing. But we relaxed and enjoyed it while it lasted, without too many illusions or excesses. I had received some gifts in cash, but was fully aware that I had a long summer ahead of me and that it would be foolish to confront it with an empty pocket.

* * *

I had indeed a lot of travelling planned for the summer.

The main object of my journey was Geneva, where I was to improve my French, but it turned into quite a continental journey, to borrow Boswell's phrase. My first stop was in Berlin, where I stayed with John Wulfsberg, a Norwegian friend, whose father was a favourite of mine, a widely travelled man who could tell the most wonderful stories of his experiences. I was under the impression that John was much quieter and maybe even a little bit boring. But I had misjudged him. During the days, while he was at the Norwegian legation, I toured Berlin, very much Hitler's capital, extolling the glories of Nazism and of military power. I went to an exhibition of modern German art — heavy-handed and Arian. It actually reminded me of Soviet art, exalting the Stachanov workers. Another exhibition was called Die Greueltaten des Bolschewismus — the horrors of the Bolsheviks — it was even worse than the SS-paper Der Stürmer that had been forced on me some years earlier. For instance, there was on display a piece of human skin, purportedly having come off the back of a maltreated prisoner. Wow! I did not realise that it could well have come off the back of a prisoner in the German concentration camps instead, which would probably have made me shudder even more. And all this a few months before the Ribbentrop-Molotov-pact was signed, an agreement that made the Second World War possible. Our world is at times a most bewildering place.

In the evenings, John took me to the Kurfürstendamm, known for its night life, and we worked our way systematically down the avenue until we had covered almost all the establishments. We did not spend much time in them, and with a sangfroid I had never expected, John would sit down at a table without ordering, ignoring the protests of the waiters and the maître d'hotel. Only occasionally would we have a glass of wine or beer. Who could afford to make a complete inventory of Kurfürstendamm if they had to pay at every place? Our motto seemed to be "to see but not to touch", and maybe that was just as well in those surroundings, which reminded me of Marlene Dietrich and her Blue Angel.

One night, John took me along to a dinner given by the legal adviser of the Norwegian legation, a German, and what a dinner! Five courses and seven different wines — it turned out that he was a famous gourmet. Not very good publicity for the Nazi slogan "guns, not butter". Afterwards at coffee, I talked to one of the other guests and we got on to the subject of music. I expressed my admiration for Bruno Walter, who had recently been conducting the Stockholm Philharmonic orchestra. I was treated to a long and enthusiastic exposition of the inestimable value of this great conductor and the key role he had played in reviving the music life of Berlin. All of this from a man who was sporting a needle in his lapel, showing that he was a member of the Nazi party. After the peroration, I ventured a little question:

—Excuse me, isn't Bruno Walter Jewish?

Which immediately resulted in an explosion:

—Ja, und welch ein Schwein er ist!

* * *

The next stop was Basel in Switzerland, where I stayed with the Scheibli family. As a young woman, Mrs Scheili had met my father in London and they remained good friends through life. I strolled around the charming old city and enjoyed the cultural life, not least the music. We went on an excursion round Vierwaldstätter Lake and passed Kssnacht, where the Swedish-born queen Astrid of Belgium had died in a motor accident — with her unfortunate husband at the wheel.

Then on to Zurich, where I stayed with other friends of my father in the suburb of Meilen. Here I was confronted with a life style that I had not previously experienced: the family got up before six and went for a short swim in the lake. Breakfast followed after which they all disappeared — the father to his job in town, the children to school and the mother to shop or to take care of other household chores. The German language radio station Beromnster closed down their morning transmission at 7.30 a.m., as apparently no one could — or should — listen after that time.

The great attraction in Zurich that year was the Landesausstellung — a Swiss national fair — and I was taken around it twice. The first time by Dr Bachmann, the head of the Central bank, a charming and cultured old gentleman. I was impressed by the fact that he took time off to show the fair to the young son of a colleague.

The second time, my guide was a younger employee of

the bank, Dr Rudi Pfenniger, whom I had already met in Stockholm, where I took him to the National Gallery (I remember having swatted up on art first, little aware of the fact that I was to show an expert around). Among the novelties on display at the fair was a small TV transmittor and he saw to it that I was interviewed and shown up on the monitors — a very exciting experience for someone interested in radio.

We had lunch in a restaurant half-way up a big tower, from which you could cross the lake in a small suspension car. We were served some kind of schnitzel and Pfenniger ordered a whole bottle of red Sion wine to go with it — good, but rather heavy. I don't think he drank more than one glass himself, the rest being used to fill up my glass until the bottle was empty. I was too young and inexperienced to say no. As if this were not enough, he ordered a Kirsch (a strong drink) with the coffee. If I had known what it was, I would probably have said no thanks. The Kirsch was more than I could take. I became quite dizzy and escaped to the terrace on the pretence of taking photos of Zurich (they came out askew, by the way). The fresh air finished me off. I dashed to the men's room, where I got rid of my lunch and most of the alcohol. Afterwards, I was able to complete the tour serenely.

Many years later, Pfenniger invited my to a meal in Stockholm — he was by then managing director of one of the big Swiss private banks. He ordered a bottle of Le Cardinal — "just the wine for you". I smiled and proceeded to tell him the story of how he had been the first one to get me drunk. Pfenniger became quite embarrassed — he had no idea of what he had done to me. But I told him not to worry in the least. It had actually been a most useful experience. I had been taught that there are definite limits for the consumption of alcoholic drinks. From then on, I knew when to decline the offer of another drink.

* * *

I then proceeded to Geneva to a family who had five children of their own and took in others as paying guests, to eke out their income. At first we stayed in their large flat in the old city. It was a lovely summer and I have delightful memories of Geneva with all its water and bridges and the Alps as a background. We then moved out to what the family called their "chateau", a somewhat dilapidated building but placed in beautiful surroundings, south of Geneva. I made friends with an English boy and we rented bicyles of the light, racing variety with several gears, which came in handy in the hilly countryside. Our most ambitious excursion was the Tour du Lac, around Lake Geneva. The first day took us through Lausanne and Montreux, all the way to Evian, the well-known spa. I remember it especially for the narrow bed, which the two of us had to share — together with a large number of fleas, as it turned out.

Next day we climbed a mountain ridge and arrived at Annecy, a delightful little place. The weather had become rather inclement, however, and as we were both wet and cold, I decided that we were going to stay at a place with a proper bath tub. This was easier said than done, as no one seemed willing to take in two dirty boys. Finally, a kind owner of a small bar took pity on us, led us up the stairs to the loft, full of junk but with a bedstead. He then brought us hot grog and a jug with hot water. After washing and changing into something more respectable, I left and soon found a room at a pension for us. Clothes maketh the man, they say.

One of the other paying guests in Geneva was a girl by the name of Emmele Chanange from Ecuador. We became more than good friends and kept up a correspondence for many years. However, we never managed to meet again.

After Geneva, I went to Paris. By now, I was getting very short of cash, and after paying in advance for my room at the pension in the Rue de l'Opera, there was not much left over. As it was my very first visit to the French capital, I wanted to get an impression of Paris by night, but how was I to achieve that with practically no money left? The matter was soon solved, though. I found a travel agency which offered an evening tour for only 150 francs — about one pound sterling in those days. I paid up and soon realised that I was getting real good value for my money. They took us to five different places, and everwhere we were offered a drink and usually also a show — Turkish coffee at Le Mosqué, a scantily clad ballet at Bal Tabarin, songs in the Quartier Latin and — the best of all — an apache dance in a small place in the working class district.

Here a young man literally threw his female partner, woman, all over the place. When the act was over, she joined our group and, selecting a young Englishman on his first trip abroad, climbed on to his lap and put her arms around him so that the poor innocent boy got quite red in the face with embarrassment. However, her partner soon turned up, feigning jealousy and brandishing a knife (all this included in the tour money). The young Englishman was by now white with fear. When we left, he rushed to the lavatory to wash away all the terrible diseases he might have contracted from such a dangerous woman.

Just that little scene was worth the 150 francs.

* * *

After Paris, I joined my mother and my cousin Maud in Perros-Guirec, Brittany, where they had spent part of the summer. The beach was good, the swimming excellent and there were some interesting guests staying at our pension. Less fascinating were the large number of fleas who insisted on sharing my bed. They seem to have a preference for me which is definitely not mutual. Fortunately, it has been a long time since I came across any of them.

We took the way home via England, and were glad to have made reservations in good time, as the war was now expected to break out any time. On the day we left for St Malo to catch a steamer to Southampton, general mobilisation had been ordered in France and the trains were crowded. The harbour at St Malo was milling with Englishmen trying to get home, and many of them had to leave their cars behind.

In London we stayed with the Misses Williams on Primrose Hill Road, for decades the family's favourite room-and-board place. We managed to get tickets for Me and My Gal, an early musical running for the third year. But London was not its usual self — one could almost hear the sound of the approaching war, and sandbags were being piled up around the entrances of temporary air raid shelters. Would we manage to get home before the hostilities started? Fortunately, we had our cabin reservations, third class. Many a first class passenger was forced to sleep in the hold, as they had not booked in time.

I knew they would be worried at home and tried to inform my father that we were expecting to arrive In Sweden according to plan, but the authorities had suspended the cable services. However, I had been a short wave listener for a long time and also checked in on radio amateurs (or "hams" as they call themselves), even starting a correspondence with one of them. He happened to live in Tilbury, where we had to catch our boat, so he came down to the docks and I could give him a message to pass on (radio amateurs had not yet been forbidden to operate). It worked beautifully: a couple of hours later, a Swedish "ham" called my father at the bank and relayed the message. My mother consequently found it easier to forgive me for all the wires on the floor at home, which had tripped her up, and all the noise constantly emanating from my loudspeaker.

When our ship steamed out through the Thames estuary, the beams of the searchlights played across the skies — it was both fascinating and sinister at the same time. In spite of the fact that I had seen the military build-up in Germany, I still shared the illusions of so many people. After all, there was the Maginot line, which could stop any attack, and the French-British counterattacks were bound to be at least equally effective. Before long, English soldiers would march through the streets, cheerfully singing "We're gonna hang up our washing on the Siegfried line, if the Siegfried line's still there". No one could as yet imagine the desperate evacuation at Dunkirk or the German Blitz of London.

We arrived without further incident in Gothenburg. We had won the race, getting home to Sweden two days before war broke out.

Chapter 6

Music

At the reception after I was ordained a priest, my father remarked that the family was rather surprised at my choice in life: "When he was younger, he did not show much interest in religion, he was much more taken up with music." That is indeed true. I have sometimes even said that I believed in music before I came to believe in God. In a letter (March 1943) I tried to explain to my parents why I had become a Catholic. Let me quote a few lines from it:

"It was only in music that I found objective truth. Its message seemed to lift itself above the concrete world, and yet it had something definite to say. What this 'something' was could not easily be put into words, and apparently only a minority really perceived it — nor did it necessarily have a positive effect on them, except when actually listening."

This was obviously written by a neo-convert, but the gist of it is still valid. I have to admit that even to-day, I have no real idea why music means so much to me. There seems to be a very personal way of appreciating what I termed "objective truth". Maybe it is a parallell experience to — or preparation for — what in the religious sphere is called transcendence, where normal boundaries between different worlds tend to disappear.

Music appreciation did not rate very high at home. The one and only time at school that my father had to suffer physical punishment was when his voice was tested for singing; the music teacher could not imagine that the off-key noise delivered by the pupil could have been bona fide. My mother did not have much of a voice, either, and her active musical life was limited to accompanying some children's songs on the piano or playing a polka on a small

accordion. We did have a grand piano, though, and all of of
us three children took piano lessons, without much success.
Sounds of proper piano playing could, on the other hand, be
heard regularly from our next door neighbour, the composer
Wilhelm Stenhammar, and from the third floor, where the
brother of my kindergarten teacher spent hours practicing,
and he did indeed later become a concert pianist.

In the autumn of 1936, I slipped on the floor on my way
to the showers in the gym hall at school. There were few
showers and many boys, so we always raced for it. That
day, I won the race, but with devastating results. There was
a puddle of water on the floor outside the entrance and the
door was partly made of heavy, hammered glass. I slipped,
and with my right arm broke the pane, cutting seven sinews
and a nerve called ulnaris. Fortunately at the clinic, a skilled
surgeon took care of me, Dr Clarence Crafoord (later to
become world famous as a pioneer in open heart surgery).
My hand was saved and the injury has not bothered me
much since then, but piano playing was definitely out —
maybe a good thing at that, at least for my teacher who no
longer had to suffer from a pupil, who was rather offhand
about practicing.

My interest in music had by then developed much faster
than my ability to perform it, and it was probably more
reasonable that I should just listen and not play. I had
been going to concerts for children but soon graduated
to the general series of concerts given by the Stockholm
Philharmonic Orchestra. I was introduced to a schoolmate,
also interested in classical music. At our first meeting, we
agreed that the most beautiful piece of music in the world
was the quartet in Rigoletto, but it did not take long before
we started to appreciate both Brahms and Beethoven, Bach
and Mozart.

There is one person to whom I especially owe my rapid
development in appreciating music and learning more about
it: Gösta Törnbom, music critic of a Stockholm daily newspaper,
Svenska Morgonbladet. We had met at a skiing resort and became
friends, in spite of our difference in age. He regularly invited
me to accompany him to the concert halls. During a whole season,
I went to almost every concert given in town, and often
joined him in his office afterwards, as he had to file

his lines before press stop. It was interesting to observe him at work, and at times, I could see my own views reflected in his reviews — it even happened that we split up and took in a concert each, whereupon he had to rely entirely on my judgement. He told me that I could borrow scores at the Royal Academy of Music and taught me to read them, which helped to increase my appreciation of music. It was a fascinating year and I learnt a lot during it. I bought a two-volume history of music in Swedish but soon started going to the public library to read more in Grove's Dictionary of Music. Mozart had become my great idol, and I copied the whole of Köchel Verzeichnis out of Grove's. At one of the most memorable concerts I ever attended, Bruno Walter was the soloist in Mozart's Piano Concerto no. 20 in d minor, conducting the orchestra simultaneously. At the general rehearsal, he turned to the musicians and said: "Meine Herren, jetzt machen wir ein bisschen Hausmusik", and that is the way it was the next evening. In spite of a packed concert hall, you had the feeling that he and the members of the orchestra were there to play especially for you.

Fritz Busch was another Mozart specialist favouring the Stockholm music lovers with his presence shortly before the war. His versions of Figaro and Cosi Fan Tutte at the Opera House were highly appreciated. I especially remember Ezio Pinza as Figaro. Those were also the golden days of Jussi Björling, still performing in his home country, and when he sang Rodolfo in La Bohème, we happily queued up to get tickets for it.

When abroad, I kept eyes and ears open for occasions to listen to music. In Germany in 1936, I was restricted to listening to it on the radio but found that much more was offered than at home. However, the family I stayed with preferred listening to military marches or operettas, rather than to classical music. In London, I managed to get a ticket to The Proms in Albert Hall with Sir Henry Wood — undoubtedly an experience, though maybe more of culture and folklore than of music. England may not have produced a great many well-known composers in modern times but they do have a wonderful living tradition of music — it is difficult to find another city offering such a wide choice of quality concerts as London.

Visting Basel in the summer of 1939, I was again able to enjoy Mozart's Figaro with Fritz Busch conducting. It was an engaging family performance: Fritz was responsible for the musical production, his son staged it and a son-in-law, Martial Singher, sang the part of Figaro. There were probably many more relatives and friends present, both in the public and among the performers, and we all enjoyed it thoroughly, getting several da capos, and one aria was sung three times. That's the way I like my opera!

The family I stayed with in Geneva engaged a teacher of French for their paying guests. I told him that having just finished school, I had no intention of returning to grammar and boring exercises. But we soon found a common interest in music history. He started with Jewish psalms, Greek and Doric tonalities and went on to Gregorian chant and early church music. Via Renaissance a-capella music and early operas of Monteverdi, we arrived at Bach and Handel, but both agreed that it was getting rather too modern, so we might as well quit and turn to the French grammar instead. This was definitely snobbish, but even today, I have a predilection for early music — the older, the better, is my motto.

Studying music in those days was quite a different matter from today. We did not have the same easy access to it through frequent performances, live or via radio and stereo discs. Records were expensive and the quality of the reproduction inferior. I owned four records of classical music: two overtures by Gluck, a couple of arias from Samson and Delilah, sung by Marion Anderson, and Mozart's Sinfonia Concertante for violin and viola, which was on four sides. Our biology teacher at school knew of my interest and invited me to join the recently inaugurated Stockholm Gramophone Club. There were members who had impressive collections, one of old Edison cylinders, another one with some 1,500 inherited records, and more that he had acquired. At every meeting, a member was called upon to play his favourite record. When it was my turn, it didn't take me long to make my choice. But I never let on how small my record library was.

Someone played a record I have never even heard mentioned since — a syncopated version of Bach's Concerto for Two Violins. If I remember correctly, Alfredo Campoli, who normally played Palm Court music in England, took the second part and Stefan Grapelli the first, with Django Reinhardt on the guitar covering the whole orchestra — the two latter being members of the popular Jazz Club de France. It was a fascinating performance.

Many first class artist had found their way to USA during the war. Thus, when in New York 1941 – 43, I had a wide choice. Let me pick just two memories from those days: a Brahms symphony with Bruno Walter and the harpsicordist Wanda Landowska playing Bach's Goldberg Variations (with Toscanini in the audience).

I obviously also listened to American music, from Porgy and Bess on Broadway to pure jazz. There was Art Tatum, who looked like a boring accountant, but played like a god. Another coloured pianist was Hazel Scott, who started out with a straight Bach Invention and then proceeded to improvise around it in a charming way. Unfortunately, she disappeared from the podium after marrying Adam Clayton Powell Jr, a Harlem pastor, politician and playboy. Jam sessions were not that popular in the early 1940's, but you could find them on a Saturday or Sunday afternoon in Eddie Condon's or Nick Ryan's, where I enjoyed many of the artists who have since become legendary. The first hour was usually something of a try out, but once they got steam up, they would offer you the most wonderful spontaneous jazz imaginable. It was almost difficult to get them to quit when the ordinary band turned up — which by the way would have little to offer that could bear comparison.

Up on 125th Street in Harlem, you could still find interesting second-hand jazz records, and then there was the Apollo Theatre, of course, with a live show alternating with the movie. When the music got going, the rhythm spread through the audience and the very building started to vibrate. Once they gave a jazz version of Gilbert and Sullivan's The Mikado, with the coloured singer and tap dancer Bill Robinson in the lead, a delicious performance.

Somewhat later I came to a war-torn London, where music — like so many other activities — had almost come to a standstill. But at the National Gallery, a daily luncheon concert was offered free and I was lucky, because there I could hear Maggie Teyte in person for the first and only time. Via grammophone records, I had previously learnt to appreciate her clear voice and admired the way she could come in on a high note with full volume and perfect pitch. Few could interpret French turn-of-the-century composers the way she did — Fauré, Ravel, Hahn and above all Debussy. At the piano was Gerald Moore, who later helped to bring the accompanist out of obscurity (and poor remuneration) into the limelight. To-day, the critics will mention them not only by name — they have come to realise that the purpose of the pianist is not solely to provide background noise, but that with their experience, they can contribute to a more mature overall interpretation. Gerald Moore was to influence a whole generation of accompanists by holding seminars on the subject in many countries, and has told his story in entertaining books.

During my years of training as a Jesuit, I was given an opportunity to try my hand at various instruments. It all started at Pullach, outside Munich, Germany. In Bavaria, a Mozart or Haydn Mass is a must for Christmas. Our student conductor played the double bass but could hardly lead the orchestra from that position, so he came to me and asked if I could stand in for him. I told him that I had never attempted to play a string instrument. Shortly afterwards, however, he reappeared with a large bass and a small instruction book. I tried to explore the possibilities of the instrument and managed to get more or less correct notes out it. By Christmas (which was not far off), I decided to have a go at it. I obviously was unable to play everything. In the slow passages, I joined in on the first and the third beat but in the fast sections, I skipped everything except the first beat, imagining that this would help to give the music some of the depth that Mozart had intended. In an orchestra, it was more important to play some notes correctly than to overreach myself and make mistakes.

The next few years of my seminary training took place at Heythrop College, near Oxford, England, and I told them that I would like to continue with the bass, but it turned out that the professor of canon law played it, so would I please try a viola instead, a more urgent need. You don't get awful overtones as easily on a viola as on a violin, but I had difficulties in handling the bow correctly because of my old hand injury. Soon a new man was put in charge of music and he decided to expand from strings to a full orchestra. Well, "full" is an exaggeration, because we were limited by the number of instruments we could find around the house. I was given an old piston trombone, which I found easier to handle than the viola.

Now we were going to perform real music! The conductor decided on the first movement of Schubert's Unfinished Symphony as a good starting point, but the score had to be adapted to the limited number of instruments at our disposal, and the shortcomings of those playing them. I was given the task of rewriting the score for all the wood and brass parts. Now Schubert's score calls for two flutes, two oboes, two clarinets, two bassoons, two horns, two trumpets and three trombones, much more than we had available. After thinking the matter over, I decided on the following solution: The second flute, oboe and trumpet could easily be left out. We had two clarinets, so I let the first clarinetist take over the upper register of the first bassoon (we did not have any), supplying the lower register notes with my trombone, which also had to double up as a second horn, an important part. Of the three trombones, the first two could be ignored but the third one was vital.

After the first rehearsals, I had to make some readjustments in my score, as there were no breathing spaces for the trombonist, doubling up as I did for two other instruments. Furthermore, it was almost impossible to keep jumping all the time from high notes, with tight lips, to low notes which required distended lip muscles. I spent many a lecture working on the score as it was rather tricky to transpose for instruments, the music of which was written in the clefs of A, D or E. I suppose it was easy to find fault with the way our performance sounded, but we enjoyed ourselves, both rehearsing and playing it in the college hall. I am sorry that since my Heythrop days, I have never again had the opportunity to play in an orchestra, or any instruments at all, for that matter.

* * *

What would life be without music? It has become almost

indispensable to me and thanks to achievements in the electronic field, it is now there at my beck and call. If I am tired, it restores my spirits; if I happen to be in a bad temper, it soothes me. Should I have difficulty in sleeping at night, I put on my earphones and let in music, setting the volume loud enough to chase away all other thoughts, yet moderate enough to allow me to relax or even go to sleep. Some years ago, I was unexpectedly asked to take over a series of morning meditations on the Swedish Radio. As I was busy with other things, I started my preparations by listening to various pieces of music, and it was around these, rather than the texts, that I created my programmes. The range of choice was wide – from Gregorian chant to Louie Armstrong's Go Down Moses, and I think it went over rather well, even though some listeners missed their normal hymns or Swedish Gospel songs.

I like music of widely different types, but there are definite limits. I find it difficult to stomach Wagner, and modern electronic music is beyond me, but then I have never made the effort to study it. Do I have a clear favourite? It isn't easy to select just a single one. In an autobiographical article in The New Yorker, Jeremy Bernstein (who normally explains abstruse physics in an intelligible manner) recalls the day he managed to invite Duke Ellington to his home. Mr Bernstein Sr, a rabbi, asked the Duke what would be his desert island choice, and got the following answer: "The Bible — and Lena Horne."

If I had to select music of just one composer for my desert island, I would not hesitate long before settling for Monteverdi. There are days when I feel an urge to listen to his music, which has both depth and variety, from seemingly simple madrigals to the majestic Coronation of Poppea or the wonderful combination of prayerfulness and grandeur of the Vespers of the Blessed Virgin (Archiv Produktion, Polydor), sung by the Regensburger Domspatzen, my favourite record, and I don't seem able to play it often enough.

Chapter 7

The First Year of the War

The Second World War broke out on the first day of September, 1939. I almost said "finally", for it had been hanging over us for a long time, like a Damocles sword. I had been able to follow the way it was building up through the press and radio, through information received from my father with his many international contacts, and from what I had seen with my own eyes on the Continent. (By the way, to a Swede, the "Continent" is everything beyond Denmark, including Great Britain, whereas to an Englishmen it means everything on the other side of the British Channel.)

My own immediate future was the one-year course at a commercial college in Stockholm, the idea being that I would later join a bank or an import-export firm. The school had a good reputation, and it was beautifully situated on the heights of the southern island of Stockholm, exactly where we had watched the sunrise a few months earlier. I did fairly well at the school without having to work too hard. We had some good teachers — I especially remember the one who taught us book-keeping and commercial law, a jovial man who was a chartered accountant. From him we learnt all sorts of ways of making quick calculations without having to write it all down (this was before the days of the mini calculators). Doing the accounts of a firm became such a realistic operation that we had the feeling of actually sitting in their offices and doing it for them. My grades were generally quite good that year — I even got a book as a graduation prize (the only one during my school years). Some of them were a bit exaggerated; most teachers knew that my father was the governor of the Bank of Sweden, and took it for granted that I knew more than I really did.

We obviously followed the war, which was creeping closer to Sweden all the time. On the last day of November, 1939, the Russians attacked Finland and it was almost, though not quite, as if they had attacked us. Many Swedes wanted us to join the Finns in their struggle, but unfortunately, it was utterly impossible to do so. The Allies had given guarantees to Finland, but these were as ineffective as those previously given to Poland. With the Ribbentrop-Molotov pact, Stalin had been given a free hand in the Baltic region. Sweden sent weapons to their neighbour Finland, even though our supplies were limited, production having been cut in the 1930's in the hope that conflicts would be solved through the League of Nations (that forerunner of the United Nations), rather than by having recourse to arms. The military authorities were also liberal in permitting soldiers and officers to sign up for the Swedish volunteer corps in Finland.

Many evacuees arrived from Finland, especially children. I recall a scene in the centre of Stockholm. The winter was severe and some men were busy clearing the snow from the roof of a block of flats. A big, icy lump hit the street with a bang, and suddenly, we heard a small child screaming, an evacuee from Helsinki, who thought that bombs were falling again. The Swedish lady acting as his stand-in mother tried to explain, to calm, to comfort him, but all in vain; the desperate crying would not stop.

The horrors of the war had suddenly been brought right into the middle of everyday life in peaceful Sweden.

* * *

On the Continent, the war seemed to have come to a standstill after the violent occupation of Poland (which, in traditional style, was afterwards divided up between Russia and Germany). The British even dubbed it as "the phoney war". However, it was only a breathing spell before the real thing.

On April 9, 1940, I had taken the tram to school as usual and there we were, some thirty students, attending a lecture. There was a knock on the door, and the caretaker poked his head in and said: "Andersson". Andersson got up and left. A few minutes later another knock but the same caretaker, now calling out a new name, and a second student left the room. Before class was over, five or six of the students had disappeared. No one, not even the professor, had asked why.

In the interval, we were informed that the Germans had invaded both Denmark and Norway. The war was really getting really close to us. We realised that Sweden was suddenly hemmed in an all sides, both geographically and politically. "When will it be our turn?" we anxiously asked, feeling that it must be just a question of time before Hitler might decide to invade us too, and there would be precious little we could do to stop him.

After lunch, I did not return to school but stayed at home, glued to my short wave radio, listening to reports and news from all over and passing the important bits on to my father and to the Foreign Office (just as I had done on the day the war broke out, as the Foreign Office did not monitor radio broadcasts at that time). Hearing Churchill speaking about the invasion filled me with enthusiasm and confidence, and I definitely approved of it when he chided the Nazis for their "dastardly attack" of our neighbours. The following month, May 1940, the Germans launched their attack on the Western front. There was no washing hung up on the Siegfried Line, and it looked as if the Maginot Line did not even exist. By marching through the Netherlands and Belgium, the Germans by-passed it and could put a wedge between the British and the French forces. It was something of a miracle that so many of the British managed to be evacuated at Dunkirk. Soon afterwards, Paris fell. Dr Hjalmar Schacht, former colleague of my father, now minister in charge of the German economy, had been against the German offensive. Now he stood on the podium in Paris, watching the German victory parade through the French capital. Hitler turned towards him with a smile and said: "Well, Dr cht, what have you got to say for yourself now?" Whereupon Schacht replied: Mein Führer, es ist noch nicht aller Tage Nacht — which could translated: Let's wait until the final account comes in.

That story was relayed to us after my father's next visit to Germany, and it was something of a consolation. But it was not often that we were given a word of comfort. It seemed as if we were at the very end of everything. Soon, Hitler would

invade Britain, and that would be it. I still fail to understand
why he hesitated. At that stage, the British were quite unable
to repel a fully-fledged German attack. Thanks be to God,
the invasion of Britain did not take place. It gave the British
a breather and a chance to produce more arms, especially
the Spitfires and Hurricanes, which helped them sustain the
heavy air attacks later that year. They managed, more or
less, to win the Battle of Britain in the air, and Hitler had
second thoughts about the invasion, at least for the time
being. Nazi power was not to triumph over the whole of
Europe, after all, and from there perhaps over the rest of
the world, too.

Sweden was by now in a desperate situation, surrounded
by the Germans. Only people with strong pro-British sympathies defied commonsense and dared to hope for an allied
victory (allied at that time meaning the British Commonwealth and nobody else). Our family decidedly belonged
to this category. As far as the Swedish government was
concerned, they managed, on the whole, to keep our neutrality intact. Cold facts forced Sweden to compromise about
certain things, but not too many, and none with fatal consequences. In the end, we came out of it with our honour
intact, and our neutrality was undoubtedly of vital importance also for our occupied neighbours, who had somewhere
to escape to and a place where the postwar era could be
planned and prepared for.

As far as I was concerned, however, I was given an
unexpected chance to leave all this and go the the United
States. During the Christmas holidays, someone had told me
about scholarships from the Swedish American Foundation.
It was really much too late to apply, but my father did not
oppose my doing so, being convinced that I would fail to
qualify. To the great surprise of both of us, I was given a
scholarship to Dartmouth College, New Hampshire, for the
school year 1940-41. The main reason for my success must
have been my youth — I had not yet served in the army,
whereas other male applicants did not obtain permission
from the military authorities to leave the country. I hardly
dared to believe it to be true, and it was by no means clear
how I was going to secure a passage to the USA.

* * *

Before leaving Sweden, I had to finish my studies at Schartau's commercial college, followed by three months at the branch office of Götabanken in Halmstad on the southwestern coast of Sweden, my very first job. It was an interesting and useful period, as it gave me a chance to learn something about banking and business in practice, and not only in theory. As an apprentice, I got a chance to try my hand in various departments, starting as an assistant cashier. My salary had been set at 150 kronor a month (roughly equal to $35 at that time), which was not enough to pay for my furnished room, food and minor expenses, so I received some extras from my father. The first payday arrived. I was sitting opposite the ordinary cashier, an efficient young lady, with some ten years service at the bank. She was unmarried and living at home, and the management apparently took that for granted, for while I received my 150 kronor, she got only 133. I have seldom felt as ashamed of myself as I did that day. The Social Democrats had been in power in Sweden for eight years, and yet there was still such blatant lack of social justice and no question of equal pay. If there had been an election at that time, and I had been old enough to vote, I would undoubtedly have cast it for the Social Democrats — much had still to be changed in our country.

The cashier, however, took it all for granted. She did not utter a single word of reproach or complaint; she continued to be just as friendly and helpful as before.

* * *

At the same time, I was struggling with the problem of how to get to the USA. Since the invasion of Norway and Denmark, Sweden was almost cut off from the rest of the world. There were three theoretical ways of travelling to the USA (which was still a neutral country): one could apply for visas to cross Germany, occupied France and via Spain reach Lisbon to take a Portuguese ship bound for New York, a solution which did not appeal to anyone in our family. The next choice was to travel via Finland to Leningrad and Moscow, then catch the Transsiberian railway to Vladivostok, cross to Japan and get a ship to San Francisco, and from there on go by rail to New England. A most wonderful trip, I felt, but my father did not agree. Apart from it being more expensive, he felt that if something happened to me

on the way, there would be precious little that he could do
to help me.

There remained one last possibility, namely to travel
through Finland, which enjoyed a sort of peace, now that
an armistice had been signed with the USSR after the so-called
winter war. Finland had been allowed to retain their corridor
to the Arctic Sea and the port Petsamo, from which a few
ships could ply the oceans with safe conduct (a few years
later, after the second war with Russia, they lost this outlet).
A shipping company offered passage for the three of us who
had obtained a scholarship to a U.S. college, but could give
no clear indication when our ship would be leaving. In the
beginning of September, 1940, we set out from Stockholm,
the train taking us through northern Sweden and Finland as
far as Rovaniemi, a bombed-out town in the process of being
rebuilt. It rather reminded me of Klondike of the old western
movies. From here, a newly built road took us all the way
up to Petsamo, and there was a fair amount of traffic on
it, seeing that at that period, it was Sweden's only outlet for
export to the U.S.A.

The mail bus took two days to reach Petsamo, with an
overnight stay at Ivalo. On one occasion, our bus got stuck
behind a lorry, which kept as much to the middle of the
road as the inebriated driver could manage, and he refused
to budge and let us pass, however much our driver honked.
Finally, a Finnish officer told our driver to approach as close
as possible to the lorry while he placed himself on the running
board with his Army pistol at the ready. He was a good shot
and soon punctured the rear tyres of the lorry, which skidded
across the road and came to a standstill. We all cheered and
waved to the driver of the lorry, who, no doubt, had time
to sober up before he got his tyres mended and was able to
continue his journey.

Arriving in Petsamo, we found our ship, Mathilda
Thordén, but the captain was anything but pleased to see
us. He had no idea when the ship was to depart — safe
conduct was needed from every nation involved and they all
kept on changing their mind. He had no intention of offering
hotel accommodation to prospective passengers and told us
to go back to Ivalo and await further instructions. There we
met other travellers, and after a week, we decided to move

to the tourist hotel at Inari, situated in scenic surroundings. This became our base for more than a month and we were lucky to enjoy a beautiful autumn there — after all, we were almost 200 miles North of the Polar Circle. At that time, a Finnish liaison officer was stationed at Inari. During our stay, the Finnish General Silasvuo, the hero who had kept the Russians at bay on the northern front during the winter war, came to Inari to meet some of highranking German officers who had came across the border from occupied Norway. This might well have been one of the first steps towards the closer co-operation between Germany and Finland, which led to the second Finnish war with Russia and a much harsher treaty for the Finns than after the winter war.

Finally, on October 22, our ship was able to leave Petsamo. The final permission having arrived late in the day, the captain chose to wait until the following morning. And a very sensible decision it was, for when we steamed out early next morning, the look-out man spotted several floating mines, which the Russians had dropped in our narrow channel. We did a slalom course among them and got out safely. Soon afterwards, a German patrol vessel from Vadsø in northern Norway stopped us for inspection. Some of our passengers, who were anxiously hoping to escape from Hitler's Europe, got into a panic, fearing that they might be taken off the ship, and a young Englishman threw his passport overboard. But once the German officers had been offered some genuine Scotch and good cigars, they let us proceed undisturbed. Having safely cleared the North Cape the captain set a course for north of Iceland, but running into pack ice, he had to change direction and pass south of the island instead. Off Reykjavik, we were checked by a British vessel and some of our passengers changed ship in order to get to England more quickly, one of them being our young man without a passport.

Mathilda Thordén was a cargo vessel with accommodation for 12 passengers. There were actually 75 of us, plus some 125 Finnish-American volunteers, returning from the winter war. They slept in one of the holds. The rest of us had to crowd into any space available. I was placed in the doctor's cabin, where a Swedish- American businessman slept in the bed, a French physician on the sofa and I and two other young men on the floor.

The rest of the trip was uneventful. After 16 days at sea, we entered New York harbour, the very day of the presidential election. Now just imagine that: spending your first day ever in New York City, standing in Times Square and watching the results together with a big crowd! It would have been almost like a ticker tape reception. It was indeed too good to be true. The emmigration authorities would not let us ashore that afternoon, in spite of our pleadings. When we landed the next morning, Wendell Willkie had lost and Roosevelt been elected for another term as president, and it was just another normal working day in New York City.

Chapter 8

Dartmouth College

I had finally arrived in the States, but much later than originally planned. All the same, I stayed in New York City for a week, having a list of people I was supposed to look up. Walking along Broadway, I saw the name Charlie Chaplain displayed over the entrance of a theatre, and judging from the cost of the tickets, I took it that he would appear in person. When I found out that it was only a film, I did not feel cheated — it was The Great Dictator, that wonderful parody on Hitler & Co, which the Swedish censors had not dared to pass, as the Germans would have protested too much. It was close to mid-November, when I finally reached Hanover, New Hampshire, where Dartmouth College is located. I was to study at The Tuck School of Business Administration, renowned as the best one in the USA after Harvard Business School. That should have been a warning to me, but with the superiority of a European, I took it for granted that the standard of education would be rather low in the States and that I would have no difficulties in catching up.

That was a great mistake. My fellow students at Tuck School had worked hard to be admitted and once there, they were kept on their toes in order to qualify for the second year and leave with a degree of Master of Business Administration. They were all older than I was, and my three months at a small bank was a mere nothing, compared to their wide experience of practical business life. Furthermore, they were all Americans and immediately understood when the professor referred to Montgomery Ward — a huge post-order firm — whereas I had no idea what he was talking about. Our course of statistics presupposed more mathematics than

I had taken at school, and so forth. On top of everything, my fellow students had been hard at it for almost two months, and I had just arrived. It would have been bad enough if I had been there on time — now it was just about impossible to catch' up. And to be honest, I did not intend to spend all my time over the books. As far as I then knew, I was to return to Sweden after a year. Before that, I intended to get an impression of life both at the college and in the US in general. Consequently, my time at Dartmouth was not a great success from a scholastic point of view, but faced with a similar situation today, I would probably act in the same way.

That does not mean that I just wasted my time and learned nothing, far from it. The standard of teaching at Tuck School was high and the courses interesting. Let me give just two examples, both from guest lecturers. One was Henry Kaiser, who had started a new car factory, and now used the conveyor-belt method to build Liberty ships, which were to help the British to survive the blockade.

The other one was a sociologist with a broad experience from the depression years in the early 1930's. He once made a bet that he would be able to get along for a whole month on just five dollars. In spite of the difficult unemployment situation, he managed to get a job shoveling coal to keep a steam engine going. After a while, he was promoted to carry an oil can, squirting oil at various parts of the machinery pointed out to him by a supervisor. He found this rather boring and asked if he could not go back to the coal shovel, which brought on loud protests from his co-workers. It was against the rules to demean yourself by freely leaving the job of a technician's assistant and return to shoveling coal. To aspire to become a foreman, on the other hand, was considered to be a good thing, even though the foreman did not get much more pay, and furthermore, was not allowed to associate familiarly with his old mates. He should keep himself socially aloof.

The professor had also been on the road in the States and made similar observations. Highest ranking on the social scale among the "bums", or tramps, were those who could get a lift with a car or a lorry, then came those who rode the freight trains and last of all the foot sloggers. If you were able to qualify for a temporary job, you also earned points on the ranking list; next came those who begged, followed by those who stole and last on the list those who stole from other tramps. (George Orwell, the author of 1984, tells of similar experiences in his book Down and Out in Paris and London. Orwell, the former Eton boy, came even closer to the real world of the tramps.)

Social conditions at Dartmouth were quite different. The college belongs to the Ivy League, i.e. they compete in football and other sports with teams from prominent colleges like Harvard, Yale, Princeton and Cornell, which to many puts them into the snob class. There is some basis for this judgement, but when I was there, there was hardly any difference between the life style of those who came from a rich family and those who worked their way through college — the latter group comprising about a third of the students. Only the odd son of a nouveau riche had to show off his wealth.

During the big college festivals, however, it was obvious that there was money around, and not only in the background. Dartmouth is famous for its Winter Carnival. In the spring, they arranged the Spring Key Dance, to which I invited a French girl on a scholarship to Radcliffe. Her father owned a silk factory in Lyons, and she came to the ball in a white silk dress of a very simple cut, which outshone all the expensive gowns of the American girls (or was it just that I did not realise that a very simple dress presupposes a really clever design and thus might cost even more?). Two orchestras played for us: a big expensive band, currently in high favour, and a second, smaller one, led by Louie Armstrong, who was somewhat neglected at the time. But when Satchmo and his boys let go, everybody stopped and listened — including the members of the first band, who even forgot to take their break.

During the spring vacation, I wanted to go to Florida to see real palm trees, something a Swede found difficult even to imagine before charter flights and commercialised tourism took over. The members of the Dartmouth Canoe Club had decided to travel to Silver Springs in northern Florida, and I was invited to join them for the ride. They turned up in an old jalopy, a Buick, which in theory had eight cylinders. A wooden plank, tied on with strings, substituted for a missing running board, and on top of the roof was a Canadian canoe, upside down. The first stop was Bridgeport, Conn., the home town of one of the boys, where we were invited to a college ball. The invitation cards called for black tie, so, suitably attired, we took the car to pick up our partners. The girls, waiting in their long evening desses, were horrified at the transport offered. But the Canadian canoe made them smile and they gracefully accepted the ride.

We proceeded down the East Coast, but not without difficulty. Our maximum speed was 50 m.p.h., and an oil leak forced regular stops at which one of us crawled under the car to fix fresh chewing gum on the oil tank. We only used midnight oil, or waste oil, when we filled up. North of Savannah, Georgia, we blew a gasket and stopped at a garage for help. They just laughed at us, so we kept spluttering along.

I gave up in St. Augustine and took a Greyhound bus, first to Miami (which I found just as lovely as I had expected) then across the peninsula and up the Gulf coast to my next destination, Pensacola, to visit a college friend. I arrived very early in the morning. There were liquor bars open, but none served coffee, so I reclined on a park bench, having put on an old raincoat against the cold. A tramp joined me, asked for a cigarette and then volunteered information about the best freight trains to jump. Consequently, I decided to have a clean-up and to buy myself a new shirt before calling on my friend, and a good thing at that, as the family lived in an exclusive villa.

When I eventually arrived back at Dartmouth, I asked the canoe people how they had got on. They had not dared to return in the old car, so they had to sell both the car and the canoe. They got $25 for the canoe and $15 for the car...

* * *

I could not count on staying on at Dartmouth College for another year. It was not just a question of money; my results were not good enough to continue for the master's degree course. A friend of mine in Sweden, who had received a scholarship for Chicago University, had been called up for military service and there seemed a good possibility that I would be accepted as his substitute.

For the summer months, my first choice was to go to
Ecuador and visit Emmele, but I did not get the necessary
financial support from home to make it possible, nor much
moral support, either. Emmele's father had an import-export
business, and she was an only child, so my parents were afraid
that I might decide to stay there (even though, before leaving
Sweden, I had made a promise to my mother that I would
return home again). I had been bothered with a persistent
cough and a doctor had recommended mountain air. So I
decided that if it could not be the Andes, let it be the Rocky
Mountains. A fellow student had suggested that it would not
be difficult to earn one's keep on a ranch for a few months.
Encouraged by my previous luck, I scouted around and soon
found a student from California, who was driving home and
was looking for companions to share his expenses. When we
arrived in Chicago, he collected $5 off me for petrol and
temporarily left me at the International House of the U of
Chicago, while he visited some relatives in Milwaukee. But
before he returned, I had been invited to act as co-driver to
a student, who was taking a new car back to her brother in
Seattle. My contribution to the expenses were to be $10, an
offer I couldn't resist.

We Europeans think of the USA as a country, but travelling
across it by car, I realised that it is a continent, and a big one
at that. Driving for almost a whole week, and covering some
2,000 miles, we passed through seven states only. The central
parts of the States are flat and a bit boring, but from South
Dakota on, it was different, with the magnificent mountain
ranges and the scenic beauty of the Wild West. In Yellowstone
Park, we had to stop for a huge grizzly bear mother, who
was standing in the middle of the road with her two small
cubs. I got out, and, most foolishly, started playing with the
cubs the way one does with puppies, offering them a stick to
pull at, until I realised that I had better see how the mother
reacted. She was now standing upright by our car, hoping
to find something edible inside. After a while, she gave up,
and we gave her a wide berth on our way back to the car,
while she rejoined the cubs. We were lucky to get out of it
without a scratch, unless we counted the ones she left on
the car. In Seattle, I was invited to stay free of charge at
a fraternity house, and I spent about a week in this city,

so beautifully situated on Puget Sound, which leads on to
the Pacific Ocean.

* * *

What I especially remember about Seattle is the fact that it is
close to Vancouver. Wouldn't that be the right place for me
to go to? The date was mid-June 1941. The Second World
War was entering a most critical stage. The British had by
now no allies outside the Commonwealth (unless you count
the lend-lease aid, which Roosevelt managed to give them,
against the will of many Americans). The fight for supremacy
in the air over Britain had continued until May that year, with
the British winning or, more correctly, managing a draw. On
the other hand, the entire Balkan regions were now occupied
by Germans and Italians, the battle for Crete had ended in
disaster, and in North Africa, Rommel's forces were not
far from Cairo and Alexandria. Hitler and Mussolini had
included Japan in their Axis pact and had furthermore
managed to negotiate a non-aggression pact between the
U.S.S.R and Japan, while the Ribbentrop-Molotov pact
was still valid. The outlook for the future could hardly
have been bleaker. Were we not, once more, close to a
total victory for Hitler and Nazism? Would I have to live
in a world run according to their ideas?

Here I was, a short distance from Vancouver. Should I not
go there to volunteer for the Canadian Air Force? Only a
few British fighter planes had stood between me and Hitler's
cruel world. What greater duty than to offer to take over the
controls of one of them, and help to fight for a world fit for
human beings to live in, and not be at the mercy of ruthless
power?

I had practically made up my mind, when, on June 22,
1941, Hitler ordered his troops to march against Russia. The
war had suddenly taken a new turn. What did the near future
have in store for Sweden? I decided to travel to Washington
and the Swedish legation to find out if I could be of any use
to my own country.

Again, I was in luck. A student, living in the same fraternity
house as I did, had to get home to Los Angeles, having been
drafted. He was driving down the West Coast and I was again
invited as a co- driver, this time for free. We did the 1,200
miles without a break and I stayed a few days with my new

friend in Hollywood. What a lovely place Los Angeles was in those days, clean and well ordered. The total population of California in 1941 was some 3½ million; today, greater Los Angeles has at least that many inhabitants, and you have to check the newspapers for smog alerts and warnings about brush fires.

My ready assets were at a low ebb and I did not even have enough money to travel by Greyhound bus to Washington, D.C. A local paper ran advertisements for shared-expenses rides to the East Coast (an illegal but apparently tolerated enterprise). I found someone who was willing to take me to Washington for only $23. I thereby probably set somewhat of a record, having paid a total of only $38 for a trip round the USA, a distance equal to ½ of the earth's perimeter. At that price, you could not expect comfort — six of us were packed into the car and crossed the southern California deserts under a blistering July sun, long before any one had heard of air conditioned cars. We stopped for sleep only one night, in Amarillo in the Texan panhandle, and took no time off to admire the scenery, unless you want to count a distant sight of Devil's Canyon in the moonlight. Oklahoma was as miserably dusty as Steinbeck had described it in The Grapes of Wrath.

We arrived in Washington late at night, so late that I did not want to call a college friend, who lived in town, so I looked for a cheap hotel. I saw one with signs offering rooms from $3.50, and I thought I could manage that, took leave of the owner of the car and checked in. The next morning I phoned my friend and, while waiting for him to pick me up, I asked for the bill. I remember the exact amount, it came to $3.93, with the phone call and local tax included. I knew that I had the three dollar bills, and then I started counting out my small change. 50 cents, 70, 80, 90, and finally three pennies. It took me down to my last penny to make it, but I could walk out of the place with my honour intact.

At the legation, they told me that the Swedish Office for Foreign Exchange Control was opening up a new office in New York City and they had actually mentioned my name as a possible employee. I was given a train ticket and some pocket money and could conclude the last bit of my Continental Journey, U.S. version, in style.

Chapter 9

New York City 1941 – 43

In 1941, you could find the Swedish Cargo Commission on the ninth floor of the International Building, Rockefeller Center. Its work was to decide on the priorities for goods to be transported to Sweden on the few safe conduct ships permitted to pass through the German blockade, which had been in force since the German occupation of Denmark and Norway. A branch office of the Central Bank of Sweden and its exchange control had been established on the same premises shortly before my arrival there. All the Swedish-owned dollar accounts had been frozen by the US authorities to prevent the Germans from using them. However, we had been granted a general licence to draw on these accounts, provided that every single transaction was scrutinised first in Sweden and then by a Swedish office in the USA, working in close collaboration with the Federal Reserve Bank.

The Central Bank of Sweden sent out one of their officials, Harald T. Magnusson, to set up the office and he was given diplomatic status as a financial councillor. His second-in-command, Ulf Barkman, had up to then mainly traded in wood and paper, but having been stationed in London, Paris and Sydney, he was fluent in several languages and had a wide experience of the world, which stood him in good stead. The two of them had travelled by the Transsiberian railway, as the safe conduct traffic via Petsamo had been suspended. The trip had not been particularly pleasant, and arriving in Vladivostok short of their luggage, they had been equipped with Russian wartime winter underwear, which bore a strong resemblance to the hair shirts worn by monks in the olden days.

On the staff of the new office were also Eric G. Lagercrantz, the New York representative of Götabanken, and Sven G. Malmberg, on loan from Skandinaviska Danken. Some further personnel, among them myself, had been employed locally.

The exchange control office in Stockholm sent us copies of all the Swedish bank orders for payment by their US correspondents. The underlying transaction had already been checked in Sweden, but we had to make further investigations to be able to guarantee that it was a purely Swedish affair, not something done on behalf of the Germans. We had to check American black lists and could make further inquiries from the US bank through which the payment was to be effected, or with the official of the Federal Reserve bank entrusted with the supervision of the Swedish affairs. He got a copy, anyway, of all the licenses we issued, and it was important not to get too many complaints, as this could have led to severe restrictions in our activities.

This might sound like a rather boring job, but I found it interesting, as I thus got an overall view of the transactions between the two countries (even if these were restricted by the war). It was less heroic than flying a fighter aircraft, but I felt that I might be doing my bit to stop the German economic warfare. After a while, we learnt to smell shady affairs, but if something really important turned up, Magnusson or Barkman would take over. It is always difficult to sort out things when some one is acting as a front for a third party. I vividly remember a case where a large German firm had been taken over by a Swedish financial wizard, but the US would not accept it as a bona fide deal and refused to permit the firm to trade or use its assets in the US, which led to a lengthy exchange of coded cables.

We often had occasion to visit the foreign departments of the big banks on Wall street. One day, I had to deposit a large check with the National City Bank. Sweden had ordered a number of fighter planes in the USA before the war and already paid a substantial deposit. When they were ready for delivery, the German blockade of Sweden was a fact and, quite rightly, an export licence was refused, as the planes undoubtedly would have ended up in the wrong hands. Consequently, the manufacturer had to return the deposit, which amounted to 4.2 million dollars. It was quite exciting having to deliver it to the bank though, of course, I could never have cashed it for my own benefit. At first, Magnusson had no private secretary and he asked me to take shorthand. I had had an excellent teacher at the commercial college in Stockholm, a stenographer in the Swedish Parliament, and I was the only one in my class to have tried for a mark above the standard pass. But taking things down in shorthand is not the same thing as typing out your notes. I got into real trouble when Magnusson started dictating in English, even though I had previously told him that I only mastered shorthand in Swedish. Having played around a bit on my own with the English system, I said nothing and continued taking notes, but they were obviously even more difficult to decipher. This had to be paid for by spending late hours at the office. Such is the price of arrogance.

* * *

Spending extra hours at the office was nothing unusual, however. It was only after I had finished my routine work that I was called in to take dictation, and writing it out afterwards took quite some time. In those days, one did not get paid for overtime, and having been employed locally, I was paid less then those sent out from Sweden. My starting weekly salary was $35. My furnished room cost $37 a month, so if I spent some $3 daily on food, cigarettes and a newspaper, there was not much left over for pleasure. The head of the Cargo Commission was quite against pay rises for those locally employed (who were in majority in his department). Magnusson, on the other hand, was anxious to improve our situation and managed to increase our salaries somewhat. Even more important was the fact that we were given the same health insurance available to the personnel of the Bank of Sweden at home. Such benefits were rare at the time and the cost of hospitalisation, especially in the USA, considerably higher than in Sweden.

When Eric Lagercrantz married, he and his wife Mary, an American girl from New Hampshire, invited me to live with them in their house in Dobbs Ferry, Westchester County. I was offered half-board accommodation at a very reasonable price, which suited me admirably. It was interesting to experience suburban life and I enjoyed the company of Eric and Mary, who have remained my good friends.

When the Magnusson family rented a villa close by, I stayed with them for a while and had to teach Mrs Magnusson to drive (a rather nerve-racking experience). But I am a typical city boy and soon moved back into Manhattan. I used the weekends to explore the various typical ethnic districts of the city: Germantown around the 86th street, Chinatown, Harlem, the Spanish-dominated district (since then vastly expanded) and many others. It was very much like going on a foreign trip. Suddenly the scene would change: signs, advertisements, newspapers were in another language. People talked Yiddish, Chinese, Spanish; the movies offered "native" films and the restaurants exotic dishes. I used to stroll around in these different surroundings and enjoyed it thoroughly, and it was all free of charge.

I got along well with my colleagues at the office and we have have kept in touch through the years. The Barkman family I knew since way back, as Ulf's father and mine had been childhood friends, and I had often met Ulf's English-born wife Ruby in Sweden. In spite of the fact that they were a bit older than I, we became close friends and they took good care of me. My last abode in New York was a minute one-room apartment on East 52nd street between Lexington and Third Avenue, but the Barkmans had the penthouse apartment and I was almost one of the family. There I met many interesting people — the Swedish artist Einar Nerman (known at home especially for his design on a match box sold for charitable purposes) and Nils Dardel, who was as eccentric as his surrealistic painting. He had been caught up by the war in North Africa, where he had produced some wonderful drawings and aquarelles of the local Arabs, but then found his way to New York via Mexico. "Some people suggest that I was scared," he commented, "but my main fear was that war might turn out to be character building." There were the two Forbes-Robertson sisters, daughters of a famous English actor, the John Gielgud of his days. One of them, Diana, was married to a well-known U.S. war correspondent. She was as beautiful as a statue of the goddess, whose name she bore, and I remember sitting on the floor looking at her in silent admiration. I believe she was the one who brought along Frederick Prokosch, whose book The Seven Who Fled I had read from cover to cover during the boat trip from Petsamo. To my mind, few contemporary authors handle the English language with the same elegance.

* * *

I liked working for Magnusson, but there was one complication: my father was his boss. Normally, it did not make any difference, and I do not think that I received much preferential treatment because of it. But it did happen that my father's friends invited me instead of Magnusson. I always asked his advice about whether to accept such invitations or not, and when I came back, I would report on the proceedings. It could occasionally be embarassing. One day, I found myself having lunch with the senior partner of a private bank and his financial expert. They thought that the Bank of Sweden should increase their deposits with them. It was not very clever to invite a 21-year-old boy for that purpose instead of Magnusson, and we both had a laugh over it.

Once, however, Magnusson could not help being a bit envious. Leon Fraser, president of the First National Bank, asked me to have a meal with him at his club together with T.H. MacKittrick, who had just returned to the USA after spending several years at the Bank for International Settlements in Basel, Switzerland, where he had had close contact with my father. After his phone call, a letter arrived, listing those invited — some forty top people from the US finance and industry, only chairmen of the board, presidents and an occasional senior vice president. I wanted to cancel my invitation and ask if Magnusson could not be invited instead, but he felt that I ought to go myself.

Fortunately, I was listed as "son of governor Rooth of Sweden" and people were very kind to me. Everyone just treated me as the son of an old friend. I have kept the list of invitations, but I do not gloat over it any more. Leon Fraser was almost retiring in his manner but very kind to me, inviting me several times to his home on Park Avenue and he also took me out to the theatre. I was most distressed to learn some years later that he committed suicide for reasons quite unknown to me.

*   *   *

After a year in New York, I tried to look forward. Finding myself, by chance, outside the German blockade of Sweden, I did have a wider choice than most of my compatriots, and it seemed reasonable to take advantage of this. Would it not be sensible to plan my future by going to Latin America at this time and gain experience and get local contacts that would be useful after the war? I tried to discuss these questions with my father, but due to the erratic mail service it was impossible to keep up a meaningful discussion. Friends suggested that Latin America might become of great importance in later years. In a letter to my father (27 April 1942), I had thrown in as an alternative that I might join the British army, which he found most surprising in the context. His only comment was: "There you would gain neither business experience or money" (30 May 1942).

In New York, I had made the acquaintance of a Russian, Elena Arapova. She had lived in Paris, a place of refuge for her parents after the revolution, but after their death, she moved to the USA. We met regularly and my feelings for her must have been rather warm, as she managed to drag me to see Andy Hardy films with Mickey Rooney, which was sheer penance for me. Through Elena, I had got to know a number of white Russians and was invited to many of their parties, crammed with princes and generals, who cherished memories from days gone by with a lot of nostalgia. One of them, after having imbibed a certain amount of liquor, used to recite Pushkin with such fervour that I thoroughly enjoyed it without understanding a single word.

Thus passed two years in New York City. They were interesting and important for me, for here I made two vital decisions: to become a Catholic and to join the British Army.

Chapter 10

How I Became a Catholic

Towards the end of my two-year stay in New York City, I was received into the Catholic Church. This was not the result of any sudden impulse, but rather the last step in a long journey.

To retrace it, I have to go back a long way. In earlier chapters, I have frequently mentioned my father and the reader has presumably concluded that he played an important role in my life. He did indeed, especially with regard to my interest in finance and business and various issues in international politics, and I appreciated him very much as a person. But in everyday life my mother meant much more to me as it was with her that I lived after the divorce.

The divorce, yes... I have so far only alluded to it and have perhaps given the impression that I would prefer to repress even the mention of it. And that is true — I would gladly do so if it were at all possible. Though half a century has gone by and both my parents are dead, it is still an open wound.

It was in the spring of 1930. My brother and I were sent to see a Buster Keaton movie. That was the last time he made me laugh, because when we returned home, our parents told us that they were going to separate, something I was completely unprepared for. I was eight and a half years old. I had never heard my parents arguing angrily nor seen anything that could have made me suspect anything of what was now about to happen. Through classmates at school, I knew there were such things as divorces, but it was quite unthinkable to me that such a thing could happen in our family. Much later on, I was told about tension in their marriage and someone described the atmosphere between them as frigid, but I had not noticed anything untoward at the time.

In those days, Swedish law prescribed a period of one year's legal separation before divorce could be granted. My father moved in with his parents and after the decree nisi, he remarried and an unusual legal settlement followed: I was to live with my mother and my older brother with father while my sister could make her own choice. She opted for dad, which was presumably to be expected from a 15-year old girl, but it was not really him she got, rather a new home with dad's new wife.

And so started all those years of being pulled in two directions. One weekend here, the next there. Half the summer in one place, the rest somewhere else. I had had one set of parents, now I had a father and a mother who lived in separate worlds and life had to be retuned accordingly. If I wanted to visit grannie, I had to check beforehand if dad's new wife was there, because in that case mother could not come. Friends and relatives of the family chose sides, and most of them opted for dad, which meant a much more restricted life for my mother. Some one else was now the wife of the governor of the Bank of Sweden. My sister and brother no longer lived with their mother, but only came to visit, and another woman was entrusted with their education, something which mother felt to be especially humiliating.

I felt that this was all wrong. I do not want to set myself up as an arbiter and make judgements about the responsibility or guilt of those involved. I admit that I was too young at the time to be able to understand. But I still do not understand, and I will never learn to accept it. There is, of course, nothing very unusual about married couples sometimes having difficulties in getting along. Quite a few years ago, there was a proposal in England to make incompatibility legal ground for divorce. Chesterton made the comment that in that case, all marriages should be dissolved, because man and woman are incompatible. Obviously, there are cases where continued cohabitation turns out to be impossible. But in our case, as in many others, it was not a question of impossiblities. They arose later, at least for us children.

It was my confirmed conviction that the divorce was just not right, even though I could not argue it out. Here began a process which would lead to questions about the meaning of life, about ethics and religion

However, I first want to point out that my attitude to the divorce was not just something that my mother passed on to me. I could indeed feel her disappointment and sorrow, even bitterness, but she was at the same time anxious not to set me up against my father or try to denigrate him. There was never to be another man in her life.

Mother and I got along excellently and I look back on our years together with gratitude. She brought me up in an atmosphere of trust and confidence and our relationship was more like that of two friends. Our home was at the same time also open to relatives and visitors, and we usually had a student lodging with us and a trainee girl from a school of social science to help out in the household.

* * *

It was not easy for me to start asking questions about life. I was too young to clothe my thoughts in words even to myself, and there was really no one with whom I could talk about such matters. We did not have any tradition in our family of intellectual discussions of philosophical or moral problems. The conversation tended to centre more around practical problems, even if these were often seen in a larger, international context.

Nor did we have a living Christian tradition to fall back on. My mother helped me to say my evening prayers, but when I was about five, I was left to do so on my own. Seeing that no one else in the family seemed to pray, I could see no reason for keeping it up myself. We were not churchgoers, with the exception of early morning service on Christmas morning, but then only if were staying out in the country and could go there by sleigh, pulled by a horse with jinglebells. In town, Christmas started with a gathering at grandmother's early in the morning of Christmas Eve. Candles were lit and then dad recited the poem "Tomten" (by Victor Rydberg, a freethinker) — a friendly gnome who watches over the household, a prototype of Father Christmas. Later, I wondered why grandmother never suggested that we should read the Gospel instead, but she didn't. She was a convinced Christian but her faith was of an evangelical kind which she did not manage to put into words or pass on to any of her children. Grandfather had decidedly outgrown the Christian tradition.

At school, I started to take some interest in religion. We were given small pamphlets to read and expound in class and I got one called Whom did Jesus want to be?, written by Anton Friedrichsen (a professor at Uppsala, at that time a liberal theologian but later renowned for his very solid New Testament exegesis). I was preparing my talk at home when mother came in and I said: "I think I am going to become a Mohammedan." My mother was more than surprised and wondered what caused such strange aspirations, whereupon I replied: "Well, at least you know that he did exist." Friedrichsen's disciples may shudder when they hear this, but neither mother nor my teacher of religion tried to correct my reading of his text.

I was prepared for Lutheran confirmation by the Rev. Erik Bergman, father of the film director Ingmar Bergman. Instead of offering us some catechetical instruction or thoughts to deepen our faith, he spent the whole year going through New Testament texts. I am afraid his comments did not make lasting impressions on me, with one exception. We had just read how Jesus had been taken prisoner in the Garden of Gethsemane and how all the apostles fled, though one young man did remain, and pastor Bergman asked us: "Who was he, according to modern research?" I used to frequent the public library and had acquired the habit of first having a look at the shelf of returned books on the assumption that if a book had been in circulation, it might be worth while reading. I had found one by an author called Wallace. I thought it would be Edgar W., the well-known writer of detective stories. It turned out to be another Wallace, however, but the book fascinated me and I was convinced that the contents were historically documented. Consequently, rather proud of myself, I proffered the name of Ben Hur. Pastor Bergman became livid with rage, quite convinced that I was trying to pull his leg, and I was given a stern reprimand, instead of being commended for having studied the primary sources.

Confirmation was set for a beautiful spring day. I cannot remember having reflected much about the communion service, but then no one, including pastor Bergman, had ever suggested to me that there was anything special about it. My

personal difficulty was rather having to recite the Creed.
What did I really believe in? I remember telling God (if He
existed): "Alright, I'll read it all, as the others do, but don't
turn up afterwards and expect me to stand up for all of it".
(Was I predestined to become a Jesuit, knowing all about a
reservatio mentalis at this early age?)

I kept asking questions in school during classes of religion
and I joined an association for Christian high school students, but I was dissatisfied with the answers I got, feeling
that they often evaded the issue. Take an example: "What
happens if I travel straight out into space? There must be a
limit somewhere, surely, and yet, what is beyond that limit?"
This was before the time of satellites and real space travel,
and Einstein's theories about the curvature of space had not
yet confused my mind.

"Well", the minister-teacher would say, "you had better
ask a scientist about that". Years later, when I met my first
Catholic priest, I asked him the same question. He scratched
the back of his head and said: "We did have a subject in
the seminary called cosmology, but I am afraid that that
was not my line. However, if you insist on an answer, I'd
put it this way: In the beginning, God created the world.
And this is when time started, and the world is as big as He
created it."

Not a very conclusive answer, but — what is there to add?
The important thing for me was that, at last, I had found
someone who took both faith and reason in earnest and tried
to see how they could fit together.

* * *

The rector of Cranemoor, the English school I attended
during the summer of 1937, had a very sensible rule. On
our way to Sunday dinner, we had to leave a letter, or at
least a post card, so that he did not have to answer inquiries
from anxious parents wondering if their children were still
alive. Having joined some fellow students at Matins in an
Anglican church, I was struck by two things: the chanting
of the psalms and an elevation of the collection in front of
the altar. So I wrote home telling my parents that the service
had been 'Catholic and therefore awful'. A few days later
I found myself thinking about that judgement. Why had I
put it like that? What did I really know about the Catholic

church? So I decided to find out more about it to be able
to judge about it myself.

Now that was not an easy thing to do. Sweden was very
anti- Catholic in those days. I did not not know any one who
was a Catholic. Of course, there was a Catholic church on a
side street near NK, the big department store in the centre of
town, but the idea of entering it frightened me. And to look
up a Catholic priest was totally out of the question. 'Watch
out for their snares', we had been told. Not yet 16, I found it
difficult to rid myself of the reactions common in a country
proud of its Protestant glories.

* * *

Then came the two months of the summer of 1939 in and
near Geneva. From the so-called chateau south of the city,
a group of us decided to make an excursion. We started at
midnight on August 2 and made for Le Reculet, a peak some
5,000 ft. above sea level. A full moon made it easy for us
to follow the mountain paths and we reached the summit
just before sunrise. Down below, we could see the Lake
of Geneva, steel grey in the pre-dawn light. Then the sun
rose. It was like a perfectly staged performance. One after
the other, the alps appeared — Dent du Midi, Mont Blanc,
Monte Rosa, until the whole range of them were spread out
in front of us.

It was not the first time that I had appreciated the beauties
of nature, but this was quite unique. I became intensely
aware of myself. On the other hand, I felt so tiny, confronted
with this impressive and resplendent display of nature. It
didn't, couldn't just happen to be there. I became intensely
aware of the fact that I was looking at the wonders of
creation. A hymn from Bedales came spontaneously to my
lips: We thank Thee God for this fair earth.

I had just prayed on my own for the very first time. Now
I knew that there is a Creator, a God. Contemplating the
beauty that He had shown me, it was obvious that God
is not just a set of physical forces. It was definitely a
person-to-person call. Until then, I had tried to find arguments to believe, but I had never come across anything
that seemed convincing. Now I did not need arguments
any longer, for I had seen His works. From that day on,
I have never been able to doubt His existence. Previously, it

had been so difficult even to begin to believe, now it seemed self-evident.

From there on, it was mainly a question of getting to know Him better.

* * *

That was going to take some time, but in a way things almost resolved themselves. I went to Mass for the first time together with my friend Emmele, but I did not find it very inspiring. The R.C. country parish situated in the midst of Calvinist surroundings had only a small wooden hut for a chapel, and the liturgy was a low Mass, without any of the polyphonic music I had learnt to appreciate. Furthermore, they still stuck to the old countryside tradition of seating men on one side and women on the other, and Emmele was probably the strongest reason for my being in church that day. Although we were very close, I cannot remember us ever having discussed religion, nor did I make any comments about Le Reculet, unless it was at the very time we were up there. But then I had been so overwhelmed that I was hardly able to utter a word.

I cannot remember trying to grapple with the question of God during my last year at home. It probably needed a period of quiet before ripening. At Dartmouth, I occasionally attended Mass but I had no Catholic contacts except an indirect one. A Swedish-American fellow student told me of his room mate, a young man from Philadelphia, who used to get down on his knees and say his prayers every evening. That made an impression on my friend, and also on me.

In New York City, I started to go to church with the help of "The Sun", a newspaper with a Saturday column on music in the churches. There I found information about a-cappella-choirs singing Monteverdi, di Lasso, Vittoria and similar composers, practically all under Catholic auspices. I thus got acquainted with Catholic surroundings, but somehow or other, I did not get around to taking any further steps on my own. One day, however, I was taken ill and was told that I had a cyst situated under the last vertebra, a minor deformity from the embryonic stage. It had to be removed and friends of mine found a rectal specialist who suggested three hospitals where he could perform the operation. One of them was St Clare's on West 59th street, and I opted for it immediately.

Here I met my first nun — and she seemed quite normal. Other nuns looked after me in the ward or during the operation, and they all seemed quite cheerful and friendly. No one tried to force anything on me. After a couple of days, the hospital chaplain, a rotund and jovial Franciscan named Fr. John Damascene, dropped by but only to exchange a few friendly words. Afterwards, I told the ward sister to inform him that I'd be glad to have him come again. When he reappeared, I spontaneously told him that I probably wanted to become a Catholic. Whereupon he replied: "And what do you have against Catholics?" I did not hesitate long: the Inquisition, indulgences and the Jesuits.

He was obviously the right man to introduce me to the Catholic faith. (The most difficult bit to get me to swallow was the question of indulgences, which is almost a four-letter word in Swedish.) We had been hard at our discussions for quite a while when he got orders for a transfer to Wilkes-Barre, Penna., and he would have liked to receive me into the Church before leaving. I said: "Sorry, Father, but I am not ready yet", so he handed me over to some one else to finish the instruction. I'm afraid that this was not a good idea, because Fr Sebastian, who took over, was a newly ordained priest who had very little experience of the non-Catholic world. He seemed to fulfill the definition of the seminarian who knows all the answers, but has not understood any of the questions. At any rate, my questions were quite foreign to him, and before long, I stopped going. It did not put an end to my interest in the Church, though, and I ploughed through many books on Catholicism, from simple apologetics to St Thomas Aquinas and St John of the Cross. But in the long run, I realised that I could not sort things out on my own, and went back to St Clare's to talk to the new chaplain, Fr. Jerome Anthony. He had been a professor of philosophy and knew how to turn and twist the answers until I got one that I could accept. After a while he suggested that it might be time for me to be received, but again I wanted to leave it to a future date. Not yet...

But it soon dawned upon me that what I apparently wanted to do was to keep on hedging, wanting to keep my freedom and be able to decide on my own which way to jump. On the other hand, I no longer had any intellectual difficulties about the Catholic faith. I did believe it all. Consequently, I no longer had a real choice, all I could do was to 'yes' or 'no'. Existentially, it was a most chilling experience. I had to say 'yes' and I felt as if the Lord was forcing me to sign a blank cheque, having no idea how many zeros he was going to fill in afterwards.

But that was not the way I felt on the afternoon of March 22, 1943, when Fr Jerome Anthony received me into the Catholic Church at a ceremony in the Franciscan church on West 43rd street, near Penn station. I went on my own, and an unknown worshipper was asked to be my official witness. My boss had given me the afternoon off 'for personal reasons' but when I informed him afterwards what I had been up to, he said: "Well, if I had known that, I am not so certain that I would have given my consent."

The next morning I attended the 8 o'clock Mass at St Patrick's Cathedral across the street from my place of work. Only the Lord and I myself were aware of the fact that this was my First Communion.

Chapter 11

Soldier in the British Army

In the early spring of 1943, I made two important decisions. On March, 22, I was received into the Catholic Church. Two weeks later, on April, 6, Magnusson sent a cable to my father, informing him that "Lars has volunteered for active service in the British Army. All attempts to dissuade him seem in vain."

It must have been a difficult period for my parents. I had written them a long letter two days before becoming a Catholic to explain my step, but it did not reach them until May, 1. By then they had been in agony during three weeks over my decision to join the British Army. It was undoubtedly a bit much at the same time, and they must have wondered what their son was up to.

Was there a logical connection between the two decisions? I am inclined to doubt it, as it was only when preparing this chapter that I realised their close proximity in time. I would rather call them two phases of development in my life that happened to converge. My conversion had deeper roots and needed long years to mature, whereas the decision to join the British Army was partially due to more immediate circumstances.

It was by no means self-evident to me to decide to take an active part in the war. Though I definitely wanted Hitler to lose the war, it had never entered my mind to sneak off to England when travelling to USA in the autumn of 1940. I considered myself a pacifist, finding it quite abhorrent to have to kill strangers, who had been ordered to fight against me. War did not seem an acceptable way of solving human conflicts.

During my stay at Dartmouth College, the skies over

Europe had become darker and the sea risen higher, to quote Churchill and Chesterton. The Germans seemed close to a final victory. Though following the news daily, I had been too full of local day-to-day impressions to reflect about the future. After leaving Dartmouth and travelling across the US continent, I had ample time to think about the world situation. In an earlier chapter, I have recounted how close I came to joining the Canadian Air Force at that time.

At the end of 1942, I was given to understand that I would not be granted further deferment from military service in Sweden, and arrangements were made to find a safe-conduct ship to take me back home. I was not unwilling to help defending my country which was officially neutral but completely surrounded by Germans. I balked at the thought of being stationed on a small island in the archipelago with orders to shoot at whomever arrived first. If I had to become a soldier, I wanted to choose sides myself.

I brought up these questions one day when having lunch with my Russian friend Elena. When she was a penniless orphan, her rich relatives in England had failed to help her and as a result, she had a chip on her shoulder about England. So she sneered: "Well, if that is the way you feel about it, you might as well join the British Army." That was all I needed to make my final decision.

In a letter to my parents I stated my case:

"I cannot stand by and look at Europe going to pieces without doing something myself. By taking sides for the Allies, I do not necessarily feel that they are wholeheartedly in the right...but the other side has to be stopped. It is not even necessarily a question of whether you like taking an active part in it; it is more a question of moral duty. To my mind...I will be helping Sweden by helping the cause of Europe, whereas I might not help it by being in the Swedish Army."

The possibility of Sweden being overrun by the Germans was by no means an unlikely one.

In a cable, my father argued against my decision, saying amongst other things that my course of action might cause him difficulties when on official journeys in Europe. I do not know how serious he was about that argument; but once I insisted on having my way, he was if anything rather proud of having a son who fighting on the "right" side. That was also the opinion of several of his foreign colleagues and he kept their letters. A Belgian friend congratulated him, suggesting that part of the credit was due to the father. Dr. Pfenniger from the Swiss Central Bank (who had been my guide in Zürich in 1939) was in New York in 1943 and we met several times. He wrote to my father the following year, telling him how he had tried to talk me out of joining the Army, but in vain. He comments: "It seemed to me that in those days, Lars was extraordinarily happy and saw his way very clearly. He was filled by some inner light, and I can only hope that it will never leave him."

* * *

When I went to the British Consulate General in New York, I was informed that foreigners could not join the British Army. They suggested the Norwegian or Free French corps, but that was not what I wanted. The United States had entered the war after Pearl Harbour, but I was afraid they might send me to the Far East. That was not my war.

It was the British Army I wanted to join, nothing else. So I went to see a friend of my father, Willy Hill-Wood, of Morgan, Grenfell & Co (merchant bankers in London), now stationed in New York as an economic advisor of the British censors. He passed me on to his old cricketing friend Rex Benson, the British military attaché in Washington. I do not know whether it was a pure coincidence or not, but some months later, Benson informed me that the rules had been changed and that the British Army would accept me as a volunteer.

In the middle of July, I was sent across the Atlantic in a huge convoy. We travelled by devious routes to avoid the German U-boats. Our ship, being in the centre of the convoy, was never threatened. After 16 days at sea, we landed in Manchester and I expected a warm welcome. But it turned out that the pass control people had not been informed about the new regulations, so I was refused entry and sent with a police escort to a clearance camp in London. While we were waiting for the escort, an over-ambitious customs official went through my luggage again and made me pay duty for some pipe tobacco that his colleague had already cleared.

They had obviously forgotten to roll out the red carpet.

In London, I was taken to the Patriotic School at Wandsworth. The name suggested some kind of indoctrination centre for enemies, but it turned out to be an old institution for children whose fathers had died on active service. They took away all our notebooks and letters and studied them carefully. In the meantime, we were kept under strict surveillance and contact with the outer world was absolutely forbidden. I was subjected to intense interrogation. They went through all the names in my list of addresses. Among others, they queried Hill-Wood, who had helped me to get accepted as a volunteer! I really do not know why, but there were Fascists in Britain, after all, and their leader, Sir Oswald Mosley, was brother-in-law of one of Hill-Wood's partners.

After a couple of weeks, I was granted official entry to Britain. Before leaving the United States, I had asked the advice of English friends about which regiment to join. A crack Scots regiment, The Black Watch, had been suggested as well as the Intelligence Corps, where I could use my knowledge of languages and my experience from the Continent.

There were two reasons against choosing the Black Watch. One was that, as an infantry man, I could easily have been shipped out East, something that had stopped me from joining the US Army.

The other reason was even more important: as a member of an infantry regiment, I stood every chance of getting involved in hand-to-hand fighting. I was not afraid to get hurt or being killed — in that case I would not have volunteered. I did feel a strong urge to involve myself personally in the war against Hitler but if at all possible, I wished to avoid being involved in actual killing of the enemy. Later on, when receiving infantry training, the worst part was a sham bayonet attack against sacks filled with straw, representing the enemy. After spearing him, you had to put your foot against the sack and twist the bayonet when pulling it out again. It evoked in my mind the picture of intestines pouring out of the dying enemy. Though I detested Hitler, I found it difficult to accept having to play such a brutal role.

To press the release button in a bomber or to activate the firing mechanism of a heavy gun is psychologically easier, because you do not have a personal relation to those you kill. Even in a general infantry attack or a concerted action of defence, you tend to shoot without reflecting much about the opponent you aim at. During my last months in the Army, a new man joined our section, and I was asked to go for a walk with him. He had been accepted into the Army at the age of 17, having lied about his age. Being a very good shot, he was trained as a sharpshooter. In trench warfare, it is their duty to study the opponents, observe their habits and find the right critical time to shoot them — which might even be when they had stepped out for a call of nature. Consequently, he had got to know his victims as individuals and had had almost a personal relation to them. Now, much later, it all came back and haunted him to the extent that he tried to commit suicide by jumping off a railway bridge. Fortunately, I managed to stop him at the very last moment.

The prospect of having to get engaged in direct violent action made me opt for the Intelligence Corps, where I hoped to be able to avoid similar situations. (And I was right: Only once did I fire a couple of shots in earnest with my revolver during the three years as a soldier. It was in Germany, not long after the armistice, and there was a general curfew during the night. I heard some one rummaging in the garden and rushed out shouting: "Halt, or I'll shoot." A man started running, so I fired my gun (aiming high, so as not to hit him) and started pursuing him. As I got closer, the same procedure was repeated again, but he got away. It turned out to be a thief visiting the neighbour's orchard for the third year running. This time, he had to leave his apples behind.)

Before being accepted for training in the Intelligence Corps, I had to submit to a very thorough investigation of my personal life. The whole procedure ended with language tests. I had put myself down for German, French and Spanish (having participated in a short course of the latter in New York), apart from the Scandinavian languages. The officer examining was a captain, who gave me an unseen text to translate immediately, followed by an oral proficiency test. I cannot remember the German text, but the French one dealt with the hauling equipment in a coal mine, something I knew nothing about in any languague. Still, my attempt at translation was accepted. The Spanish one, with highly technical details of gas warfare, was definitely beyond me, and there was no oral test. The officer did not bother me with translations from Scandinavian texts, but he thought it would be interesting to hear my spoken Danish and Norwegian. His accent was perfect, mine was not. In other words, here was a man who spoke at least six languages like a native, and I had the feeling that he could have kept it up if I had filled in an even longer list. Since that day, I have been careful about suggesting that 'Englishmen don't know foreign languages'.

There were five of us who took the train from London to Glasgow for a ten weeks' course of primary training. We were billeted in the old, run-down Maryhill Barracks. There were two large halls per floor, each housing 52 soldiers, so there were 104 of us scrambling to get to one of the seven small washbasins in the morning. You had to get used to the discipline, the roaring commands of sergeants on the drill-ground, meaningless routines and hanging around for ages. We had to line up at every place and soon learned patience. On the boat across the Atlantic, I had shared a cabin with John, the son of the film director Herbert Wilcox, and now we were recruits together. John, a trained camera man, was very musical, and you could find him lying on the top bed in the barracks, reading a score, while the recruit in the lower bunk was an illiterate.

At the end of the course, we were posted. I was offered a commission, which would have meant infantry and probably Burma, so I stuck to the Intelligence Corps. They sent me to North Wales for three months of infantry training. For my own part, however, it all started with having to report sick with a case of housemaid's knees, which might sound funny but was nothing of the sort. I was sent to the Bangor and Angelsea hospital in Bangor, with 33 beds in the ward. Everyone spoke Welsh, except myself. Every one had visitors who brought extra rations for them, but no one came to see me. I had acute pain in both groins and did not know why (it turned out to be a hidden abscess).

The first evening, an old patient was moved down the ward. Relatives and a minister came to visit, but soon curtains were placed around his bed and nurses and doctors took over with intravenal treatment. At one thirty in the morning, the patient was wheeled out, feet first.

The next evening, the same procedure, but another patient. He died at one o'clock. I was beginning to wonder when it would be my turn. I spent 17 years abroad without interruption, but this was the only time that I was homesick.

After the hospital, I was sent to a convalescent depot near Stoke-on-Trent to get into shape again. It was wintertime and arriving there, I saw Nissen huts on the wet slopes and soldiers in scant gym dress exercising in the mud. Not a very pleasant prospect for the near future. Fortunately, I immediately found a member of the Intelligence Corps who had been there for a while and he fixed me up as a teacher of French, so I spent the following three weeks in the education barrack, until the sergeant-major found out that there was no one taking French. By that time I had learnt to fend for myself and I was transferred to the company office as a supernumerary clerk.

Back in North Wales, I was stationed at Rhosneigr on the Island of Anglesey, where we crept along the dunes in denims, raced over battle courses and marched for hours on end. Many of us were used to sedentary jobs, and, being of an average age above that of the normal recruits, we found it tough going at times. Our average level of education was also higher, however, and this saved us. Between training passes, there was a prescribed break which started with question time. If we felt that the NCO:s had pushed us unnecessarily hard, there would be a spate of questions, very polite and to the point, but clothed in terms which were quite unintelligible to the regular soldier in charge. If, on the other hand, the pace had been more reasonable, there were no questions at all and ample time for a smoke instead. The soldiers training us soon caught on.

An Irish recruit started a campaign to make all the Catholics more active — there had to be a number of them among the Inniskillins, the regiment from Northern Ireland training us. We approached everybody tactfully. No one seemed to object and we found that both the sergeant major and the colour sergeant were Catholics but had not practised for years. We got them all to Mass and, with the exception of a half-French recruit, all the Catholic soldiers at Rhosneigr did their Easter duties that year. The credit for it must go to the priest serving us, an English Oblate father, whose name I fail to recall. He was of poor health, and one felt embarrassed on his behalf, as he could neither formulate nor develop his ideas in a sermon. He was probably the worst preacher I have listened to. And yet there was such an aura of goodness and charity around him that even the old soldiers were moved by it.

I cannot help but make a comparison with Msgr Fulton Sheen, the famous US preacher, whose Lenten sermons I had followed in St. Patrick's Cathedral, New York City. You came out of church feeling that this was the most perfect sermon you had ever heard. But how much of it did you remember? The same Fulton Sheen came to Stockholm in 1962 to preach at the consecration of the new Catholic bishop, John E. Taylor, an Oblate priest from the USA. We had rented the Town Hall for the ceremony. Fulton Sheen came up to the microphone to deliver his sermon. Before starting to preach, he stretched out his arms and looked up towards the top corner where the television cameras were located, remaining in that position just a bit too long. It took away much of the effect of his sermon.

* * *

Our next stop was the regimental headquarters of the Intelligence Corps, located in Wentworth Woodhouse near Rotherham in southern Yorkshire, an enormous building with 12 ornamental doorways and 365 windows, but we soldiers were billeted in the loft above the stables. The first three weeks stand out in my memory as one of the most enjoyable periods of my life. It consisted of a motor bike course. We were asked if anyone had any experience of riding motor bikes and I put up my hand, even though I had only ridden on a pillion. The first day, we had to get familiarised with the equipment in general and especially the foot gear, a recent technical innovation. We were also taught how to fall off a bike without getting hurt. The following day, we of the "elite" class started taking trips all around the countryside, whereas the others had to spend a whole week just touring the grounds. Our teachers were professional dirt track riders. They had us driving along major roads, up and down the huge slag heaps situated near the coal mines, and on muddy, steep trails through the forest, almost like the modern trial or enduro. I relished it all and felt almost as carefree as during the weeks after finishing school in Sweden.

But life at Wentworth was not all beer and skittles. We were put through hard training by the tough Grenadier Guards, and they were not as easily fooled as the NCO's at Rhosneigr. We had to run until we were ready to drop, and then had to sprint the last bit. Every day, there was a thorough inspection by the regimental sergeant major, and woebetide the recruit who had not spent enough time on spit and polish.

From Wentworth, we were sent to Matlock Spa in Derbyshire, where a hotel had been requisitioned. We were taught specialised intelligence work such as security control at military installations, interrogation of prisoners of war, port security and similar matters. Our teachers were highly qualified and good pedagogues at that, using all their own practical experience and knowledge of languages to make things more interesting. I especially remember them staging a typical scene of life in port security. It started with them rowing out to the ship, then climbing the rope ladder, checking the captain's papers and the ship's log and cross-examining suspect sailors, who kept jumping from one language to another, when you put on pressure. It would have received top rating as a television entertainment programme.

Chapter 12

On Active Service in Europe

Our general training in the Intelligence Corps had now been completed and we were sent to London to await posting to various units. The allied invasion of Europe had started on D-day, June 6, 1944. It had met with greater resistance than expected and it was not until D + 63, or August 7, that it was our turn to be shipped to Normandy. We travelled through the British Channel on a large ship but changed to landing-crafts to get to the beaches. Large tents had been put up for us in a typical Normandy orchard. It was a very hot summer and we were plagued by swarms of wasps. They also spread a kind of dysentry we nicknamed Normandy sickness, and I was struck down and had to spend a week in a field hospital. There I made friends with a soldier, who was under arrest. He was a professional cameraman at Ealing Studios and, having been drafted, he ended up in the Army Film Unit. The commanding officer of his group was a captain, who had been in charge of the pay office at Ealing. He had had the machine gun taken out of a tank and replaced it with a camera, and my friend was ordered to join the attack against the Germans to get good, vivid pictures. He panicked — a most natural reaction — and was put on a charge for refusing orders under action. Now he was waiting for his court martial and could get a heavy sentence. War makes you cruel, even to your own people.

The allied forces had not yet succeeded in piercing the German defence lines and we were enclosed in a small zone. Occasionally, we could hear artillery duels, but there were no German air raids against our camps. We did not have much to do, so a Catholic chaplain collected a group of soldiers, who, like me, were recent converts and had not yet been confirmed. We were presented to the Bishop of Bayeux, who gave us the sacrament in his private chapel. Afterwards he treated us to a good bottle of wine from his private cellar. I was the only soldier who could speak French, and when the chaplain informed him that I entertained ideas of studying for the priesthood after the war, I was immediately invited to join his diocese, as they were short of vocations. I replied that they were probably in a much worse situation in Sweden, so that he should not count on me.

The break-through at the gap of Falaise came soon afterwards and the allied forces advanced rapidly. Together with another soldier, I was posted to the 90th Field Security Section, at that time attached to the 79th Armoured Division. An officer drove us to the site of a prisoner-of-war camp, convinced that we would find transport from our division at such a place. But the camps had all moved northwards, and he just let us off along the main road, telling us to use our intitiative: "The divisional sign is a triangle with a bull's head. You are bound to find it somewhere near the front."

There we stood, looking rather forelorn with all our equipment and no transport, and it was by no means easy to thumb a ride. Finally, a column of heavy lorries taking jerry cans full of petrol to the front took mercy on us. The drivers kindly shared their rations with us, otherwise we would have had nothing to eat. We kept looking for the bull's head, but without success. Finally, we found ourselves in the eastern part of Belgium, with heavy guns along the road, shelling the enemy over our heads. War was getting a bit too realistic for my liking, so we got off and found a divisional HQ, and their intelligence officer managed to locate our unit. It was in Aumale, near Arras in northern France! He arranged transport to take us to Brussels, where the Intelligence Corps had taken over the Grand Hotel in Boulevard Adolphe Max, and we soon found ourselves installed in a luxurious double room and we were well fed in the dining room, while the message went out to our unit to send up transport for us.

The following day was the first Sunday after the liberation of Brussels, so I went to St. Gudule, the major Catholic church in town, to attend Mass. It was a great and joyful celebration: a solemn High Mass, Te Deum and a sermon by the famous Msgr Cardijn (later to be made a cardinal). Only one thing was missing — they had forgotten to invite the allied forces to participate. I was the only person available dressed in a British uniform, so they grabbed me and placed the acting sergeant (really only a lance corporal at the time) among the high prelates near the high altar. There I had to represent the whole of the Allied command (which was in blissful ignorance of the role I was playing).

Brussels continued to fête any one in uniform, and we lived like princes for a couple of days. When we finally arrived to Aumale and our unit, the captain in charge of it found it difficult to accept that the two stray soldiers were not responsible for the whole outing. But he could not do anything. We had, after all, only followed orders and used our initiative.

* * *

I was now a member of the 90th Field Security Section, consisting of one captain, one sergeant major, a batman-driver and some ten sergeants. That is to say, we were not really all sergeants, even if we wore three stripes. The newcomers were either lance corporals or corporals. Still, the rank really gave the wrong impression. The sergeants were the ones who did the actual job, the captain and the sergeant major being in charge of administration and paper warfare. During the performance of our duties, we usually had to deal with persons of the rank of major or lieutenant colonel, and frankly, I considered them my equals.

If you ran into an regular officer of the old school, he might throw his senior rank at you. There was an easy way out of that difficulty, namely using the phone and putting on a posh accent. Then they immediately called you "Sir". In the summertime, you could dress in 'short-sleeve order' without signs of rank, and be invited into the officers' mess. (The US Army solved the problem in a better way by not giving any ranks at all to the members of our equivalent, the Counter Intelligence Corps. They were just called "agents" and as such had access to both the officers' and the NCO's mess.)

In Aumale, our section was attached to the Military Government and in charge of security. Our most difficult job was to find out who was a genuine member of the so-called

Armé blanche and who wasn't — the underground men
with a white armband, who supposedly had fought against
the Germans. Some of them had undoubtedly risked their
lives in the right cause. Others put on the armband to cover
less laudable contributions towards the liberation, or did it
just out of political ambition. We were soon moved north
to Hazebrouck in the French Flanders, an area previously
known to me only through ficton. When I had to go to
Lille to arrest the mistress of the German commandant of
Hazebrouck, I found her in a small furnished room with the
same stale atmosphere that I had encountered in Simenon's
books. By the way, our section got a very enthusiastic welcome in Hazebrouck. Someone had arranged for us to be
billeted at the hotel Gambrinus, which had up till then been
the German soldier's brothel. They had not had time to move
the girls out, who were delighted by our arrival.

Talking about brothels, I once made a personal, off-duty
visit to one of these institutions. Members of our section
occasionally were given short leave in Brussels and I went
there with two soldier friends. One of them was very anxious to go to a brothel, whereas the other two of us were
uninterested. He insisted, and we resisted, until finally he
said: "What is your trouble? Downstairs, it is like any other
bar, and all you have to do is to order a drink while you are
waiting for me." We gave in. He soon found a companion
and disappeared upstairs, while we had our drink at the bar
and talked to the other six or seven girls hanging around.
They found our behaviour most unusual and could not
understand why we were resisting their temptations. Finally,
one of them got frustrated and turning to my friend said:
"What is wrong with him? Why did he come here? Is he not
a man?

My friend (who was not a Catholic) looked at her and
commented: Pas pendant le carême — not during Lent. She
turned to me and asked: "Are you a Catholic?". I said yes,
and immediately, all the girls gathered around me and started
discussing the catechism, which they knew better than I did.
From that moment on, I was a guest in the house, not a
prospective customer.

The 79th Armoured division was not a tactical unit but
a specialised one with secret weapons. The most important

one was an amphibious Sherman tank, weighing all of 30 tons. With the help of tarpaulins, fixed to movable metal frames, it could float. The officer stood on top of the tower and steered it with the help of a rudder. The idea was good, but their performance on D-day had been anything but successful and further training was called for. It was the duty of our section to ensure that the existence of the tanks remained a secret. An area in the Netherlands, south of the Schelde estuary, had been evacuated for this purpose, and we had to stop unauthorised persons from entering it. During the training periods, smoke screens were laid on to prevent enemy observations. The area was just inside the dykes, which protect the low-lying country against the sea. Driving around it on a motor bike was anything but a pleasure, using muddy lanes which had been churned up by the heavy tanks. In charge of this special equipment were members of a famous lancers' regiment, but I am afraid that they were most inefficient. When they were used in the crossing of the Schelde, they made the same mess out of it as in Normandy and hardly any of the tanks could be employed in the actual attack on the enemy forces.

Our section was subsequently moved to Antwerp, where we experienced the last winter of war — and the so-called Rundstedt offensive. The allied forces became bogged down in trench warfare in the Netherlands and eastern Belgium. Quite unexpectedly, a German attack was launched against the Liège area. If they had continued northwestwards, they could have cut off our forces on the northern front and things might temporarily have become quite critical. Fortunately, the Germans instead moved towards the Ardennes, where they were eventually stopped, to a great extent through the valiant efforts of US forces. A rumour had it that a US military policeman, who was on duty, directing the retreating allied forces, had sent the Germans the same way instead of having them proceed westwards. As the Germans had parachuted men dressed in US army uniform, they thought it was their own man directing the traffic.

Antwerp was subjected to massive air raids at this time. There were only a few bomber planes, but ever more and more of V1's and V2's coming in almost every quarter of an hour, night and day. V2 was an early type of rocket, which made a big bang when it hit the ground and formed a large crater. Unpleasant, but if you heard it falling, you were all right. I found it much more difficult to take the small V 1 missiles, which flew at a low level and sounded like a moped without a silencer. When the engine started to cough, you knew that it would soon hit the ground. Its effect was mainly lateral, so you had to take cover immediately in order to avoid getting hit by glass splinter flying around.

It was a nervous time, and twice, I only just escaped. I had arranged to go to the cinema with a friend. I wanted to see a certain film, but he had already seen it the night before, the reason being that he had postponed writing his weekly letter to his wife, as there had been no mail, due to a prevailing fog. I did not insist on him seeing it again, and soon blessed the fog, because during the show, we heard a terrible blast close by. When leaving the cinema, we saw injured people streaming by. They had seen the film I had wanted to go to, and a V2 had struck right in the middle of the theatre, killing hundreds.

Another day, I heard an explosion, as I was approaching the centre of Antwerp on my motor bike. A V 2 had struck at the crossing of two main streets. The body of the policeman on traffic control was later found on the roof of a tall building. The time was a few minutes after noon, and rows of people had been waiting to cross the street, having come out of the office to go to lunch. Many of them had been killed and badly mutilated. The others just stood there, too dazed to help or run away. I saw the shrunken and charred remnants of four soldiers in a jeep. The mains of the water supply had been damaged, creating a large puddle, and I saw something floating around. I fished it out of the water and found my hands full of human entrails, still warm.

The German offensive soon petered out, and our section was moved to the river Meuse, where another and more efficent crew took over the amphibious tanks, again training in an enclosed area, controlled by us. Towards the end of March, I accompanied their transports to the Rhine, where they were to participate in the final offensive against the Germans (and they did much better than their posh predecessors). While waiting for the attack to be launched, I spent the night in a slit trench. That was the nearest I got to real action during the war.

On the way there we had had to stop a while because fieldmarshal Montgomery, 'Monty' had arrived to talk to the troops before the attack. Thousands of them had been alerted, and the area was closed because nothing was to disturb Monty's pep talk. Before reaching the place where he was to speak, he was met by soldiers who attached ropes to his car and pulled it the last bit. That was something the Desert Rats had done spontaneously after the battle of El Alamein, and since then, Monty wanted to have it that way every time. He has been subjected to a certain amount of criticism by some biographers, and I can attest to the fact that his vanity did not make him particularly popular with the soldiers. Lord Alexander was much more of a soldiers' general.

As soon as the attack across the Rhine started, I returned to Belgium, where I had spent the last six months. It was a country that I had learnt to appreciate. When asked where I came from, I always answered: "From the country of Queen Astrid", which opened every door. This Swedish princess, who had married Leopold, had become most popular, and you could find a photo of her in almost every window in Belgium at that time — she had become a symbol of patriotism and of Catholicism.

Here I must relate a story that one of the Jesuits in Sweden told me years later. He had been approached by Astrid when she was a princess of Sweden and the fiancée of Leopold's. She came to our parish in Stockholm and told the priest that she wanted to become a Catholic. Fortunately, she met the right man, Fr. Ansgar Meyer, who asked her why? Well, she said, I am going to get married to prince Leopold, become the crown princess of Belgium and later queen of a Catholic country, so it seems reasonable for me to join that church. Father Meyer asked her if she had any other reasons or if she had studied the teaching of the Catholic Church at all. When he got a negative answer, he told her to leave things as they were. If later on, she were to take a personal interest in the Catholic Church, she could always ask someone for instruction. As it was, Astrid did later contact a priest in Belgium and became a convinced Catholic. If she had been received before the marriage, she most likely would have become just a nominal Catholic without much interest in religion.

* * *

On April 30, 1945, Hitler committed suicide in his bunker in Berlin and a week later, the armistice was a fact. Our section was now permanently attached to the Military Government in the British zone of Germany and transferred first to Ahaus, near the Dutch border, then to Iserlohn, south of Dortmund. We had two major tasks: to find and arrest leading Nazis, and to vet persons who applied for posts in the administration of the new and democratic Germany that was being built up.

The prominent Nazis had all left home, but we would hear rumours about their hiding places — after all, not every German had been pro-Nazi and many of them had suffered under Hitler. They had been living in a state which kept all its citizens under strict surveillance and even encouraged children to inform on their parents. No wonder that some of them now helped the Allies to find the worst exponents of the Nazi ideas. There were many tip-offs to check out and sometimes they paid off. We located the former chief of police of Dusseldorf, a high-ranking SS officer, hiding together with his girl-friend and her mother, but he committed suicide before we had time to interrogate him. The last Gauleiter of Westphalia had gone to stay at a farmer's house in famous Hameln — the place with the Pied piper and the rats. His wife tried to hide some capsules of poison in the pocket of his overcoat.

But most of them were smaller fry. I remember a minor official of the SS; he was one of the few that seemed to be an idealist and he was convinced of the truth of his cause, even in defeat. Many others could be dubbed opportunists, and I was surprised at the number of elementary school teachers in this category — they must have had a inferiority complex which was compensated for by advancement with the help of their Nazi affiliation.

This element of opportunism became evident when we had to vet candidates for posts in the new civil administration. Every one had to fill out a Fragebogen, giving an account of his past life, especially during the period 1933-45, listing membership of political parties, affiliation to the Nazi organisations etc. We tried to check the information they had given us and, if necessary, called them in for questioning. There were standard rules governing who should be accepted and who rejected, but fortunately, we had the possibility of making personal judgements also. This process was called Entnazifizierung, that is sorting out Nazis and eliminating them from the immediate sphere of influence in post-war Germany.

It was a painstaking and often difficult job, but interesting. I had occasion to vet thousands of persons and I tried to talk to them personally, if I had any doubts. When I confronted them with their involvement during the Nazi period, I usually asked them: "Why?" (just as I later often ask people in the confessional the same question if they accuse themselves of anything serious). Normally, their explanation was more or less obvious. It had started with a small contribution to the Winterhilfe, the Nazi charitable organisation. Next year they would give a bit more, and then came the question: "Won't you join the party, we expect that of people working for the local administration. If you want to be promoted, you have to show a bit of good will. If you won't let your children join the Hitlerjugend, they will not be eligible for higher education." Or they might have been approached by friends, saying: "Please accept the post as head of our local party organisation. If you refuse, we will get a convinced Nazi holding power over us." And so forth.

Getting to know many cases from the inside, I became more careful in my evaluation. This did mean accepting any and every excuse, but I could more easily understand the situation in which they had made their decisions, and I had to ask myself: "How would I have acted in similar circumstances? Would my personal political and ideological conviction have been strong enough to resist all the pressures and ignore taking into account the consequences for my family and my own future?"

In certain cases, the end result of such continued pressure might mean active participation to a degree that the person involved was not prepared to excuse later on. They might have been ready to sacrifice much, even everything, if they could have envisaged where it would all lead to. But it had, after all, started with minor, seemingly unimportant compromises, and step by step, they had got more involved. It would have been difficult to stop half-way and say no. "You have been a member of the party for several years now, you have accepted such and such a function, how can you suddenly start being awkward?" You were caught in a net.

Compare this with the situation in the former Iron-curtain countries. They were subjected during a much longer period to the rigours of a one-party system of the Stalinist variety. They are subsequently having great difficulties sorting out those who can reasonably participate in the running of a new democratic state from those who were communist supporters either out of conviction or because they were willing to cooperate with all sort of things just because it was more profitable.

* * *

The rumour spread that there was an active Catholic in Iserlohn handling denazification, and soon there was a queue of priests and laymen asking me to put in a word for people whom they considered good and honest, in spite of the brown taint of their reputation. Among those visiting me, more than one had spent time in a concentration camp, but it had affected them in different ways. Some of them had managed to get through the past so that it had even enriched them and made them very mature. Others (and I am afraid there was a priest among them) had only kept their hate, or the egotism, which they had had to develop in order to survive life in the camp.

What happened to the Nazis that were arrested by us? They were interned, sometimes in a former concentration camp. Our section had to deliver our prisoners to Recklinghausen. It had not been one of the worst camps, but it certainly was not a pleasant place. The British warders there showed me the former correction section, used by the Nazis, with small cells of asbestos cement in the centre of a hut. "Try it out for yourself", they suggested. I closed the door of a cell from the inside and they switched off the lights in the corridor, telling me that I could come out whenever I felt like it.

The was not much room inside the small cell with a low

ceiling and narrow walls. I stood up, I sat down; there was
not enough space to stretch out. I am normally not plagued
by claustrophobia, but this time, it felt as if both the walls
and the ceiling were closing in on me to crush me. But shame
on him that gives up! I stuck it for quite a while before I
left the cell to join the others. They immediately asked me:
"Now, how much time do you think you spent in there?" I
suggested four or five minutes. They had timed it – exactly 27
seconds. How long would I have endured it before starting
to scream?

In these camps, there were military tribunals meting out
punishment. As it was, some got off lightly due to lack of
evidence, others got longer sentences. Later on, German civil
justice took over, but it did not function well. It is not easy to
achieve justice in this world, least of all after such a period
of chaos and arbitrary judgements.

Talking about justice, it was supposed to be meted out in
the Nuremburg trials. It was no doubt reasonable to try those
who had carried the greater responsibility for the war and
the atrocities. But was it equally reasonable to have Stalin's
representatives on the judges' bench? Even the allies had had
their moral reputation tarnished by the saturation bombing
towards the end of the war. I found it difficult to watch
the huge squadrons of planes flying in over Germany every
evening without getting a bad conscience. Smaller planes flew
in first and with the help of flares marked a triangle, inside
which the bombers were to drop their cargo consisting of
heavy explosives and of phosphor bombs. In Wuppertal,
some 40,000 persons were said to have been killed in a
single night's raid. Many of them became living torches
and in desperation, they threw themselves down the high,
steep banks of the river Wupper. And this at a stage when
the war was almost over.

A few months later, atom bombs were dropped over
Hiroshima and Nagasaki. Could such actions be morally
justified?

I have never for a moment had qualms about having joined
the British Army. Previously, I had been more of a pacifist,
but became convinced that Hitler had to be stopped. Today,
I would no longer call myself a pacifist, as I consider that
people have a right to defend themselves — and at times

a duty to defend others. But I would still warn any one about the dangers of becoming a soldier on active service because of the conflicts of conscience that he might come up against. All too often, wars are fought using means that are not justifiable. The individual soldier has little or no influence over such choices, his is the duty to obey and to serve. If the case should arise where he feels he must object, his attitude might have disastrous consequences for himself.

I had myself occasion to refuse an order. It was not common that our methods of interrogation became too harsh, so I was surprised when one day I entered our offices and found two Germans hitting a man they had fastened to a chair by means of handcuffs. I was furious, stopped them and immediately got hold of the sergeant responsible. The victim was a Communist, who had been in a concentration camp years previously but had been released. The people maltreating him were also Communists, who accused him of having been an informer to the Gestapo. It was a fact that those released had to sign a paper promising to bring unlawful acts to the knowledge of the authorities, but it seems that in many cases it had remained a pure formality.

Whatever the truth in the case in question, I protested against our people permitting the man to be subjected to such brutal treatment. The captain in command of our section being away, the matter was handled by the sergeant-major, who was pressured to decide that the man should immediately be sent to Recklinghausen, and that I was to take him there. I refused, even though he threatened to have me court martialled. When our officer came back, someone else had taken the poor man to Recklinghausen. A preliminary judicial investigation was held by the captain in private, and he eventually suggested a compromise that I could accept and the case was dismissed. He knew that I was not out to create difficulties and that I at the time was waiting for my release papers and permission to enter the Jesuit order in Germany. But if I had had a less understanding commanding officer, I could easily have spent the next year or so in a military prison (very unpleasant institutions) followed by a dishonourable discharge from the Army, which might well have created difficulties for me in later life.

* * *

When the situation in post-war Germany became more settled, the military government decided to permit some political activity. It was our task to check the background of prominent members of the parties and survey the way they acted and expressed themselves in pamphlets, booklets and at political meetings. I found this interesting, especially when it took us out of local politics into the regional or national sphere. When our section was moved to Dortmund, we had quite a number of political personalities visiting us and we used to invite them to lunch — Adenauer, Schumacher, Ollenhauer and others. Adenauer tended to be aloof and condescending whereas Schumacher, the leader of the Social Democrats, was a fiery spirit, which no one had managed to quell, not even in the concentration camp. His successor, Ollenhauer, was a former school teacher and at this time regional party chairman, but we felt that he had difficulties in filling even that post. I had a much higher opinion of another leading Social Democrat, Walter Freitag, who reorganised the labour unions. Unfortunately, he died within a few years.

Personally, I had a soft spot for the small Zentrum party. In the Weimar republic and earlier, it had been a Catholic party, but now, it had missed the boat. The Allied Occupation forces permitted only four parties, the Christian Democratic Union (CDU), the Liberals (FDP), the Social Democrats (SPD) and the Communists (KPD). CDU varied much from region to region. In a Catholic district, they could be compared to the old Zentrum, whereas in Protestant surroundings, it was often more conservative. Consequently, Catholic politicians with a strong social ethos wanted to resurrect the Zentrum party, but it took them a long time to get offical recognition from the military government, where the higher-ranking officers normally had scant interest in Catholic viewpoints.

Some Zentrum supporters came to see me, having heard that I was an active Catholic. Iserlohn, where our section had its HQ, is situated in a predominantly Protestant district as a result of the the rule laid down at the Treaty of Westphalia (1648): cuius regio, eius religio — the secular ruler decided what his people were to believe (a most curious way of looking at religion, to my mind, but there it was). Thus very few of the leading CDU men in Iserlohn were Catholics, and some of them only nominally so. The CDU was quite conservative, and the FDP had strong backers among the owners of small-scale industry. During the Nazi era, denominational schools had been abolished, and now the Catholics wanted to start them again. In the local political forum, the CDU and FDP vote went against it, whereas the Socialists and the Communists voted for it, at the instigation of the Zentrum party. This type of coalition was theoretically impossible but showed that the Zentrum stood for centre-left ideals.

Once, I got into trouble because of my sympathies for the Zentrum. I visited the chairman of the CDU for the rural district of Iserlohn, a diehard Lutheran from East Prussia, now living in Menden (where the Catholics were in majority). We got into a theological argument and he quoted Luther about the Catholic Mass, calling it a "scheussliche Abgötterei" — a repulsive form of idolatry. In confidence, I mentioned this quote to a Catholic priest in Iserlohn, who immediately passed it on to the local Zentrum party. Next time up for the quote was a Zentrum meeting in Menden, which caused the CDU chairman to blow up. He replied to the accusation at the next meeting of his own party, talking about a "Swedish Jesuit who had wriggled his way into his home", and he then made a formal complaint to the Military Government about my behaviour. I was summoned to higher authority to explain myself but they were not upset and let me off. I must admit that I felt a certain amount of satisfaction when, later on, I learnt that the very same man had had a Nazi past in East Prussia and that was the end of his career in the CDU.

In Dortmund, I got to know Helene Wessel, who had been active in the Zentrum before 1933. She asked me to intervene with the Military Government in order to get a more reasonable allocation of news print for their party paper, the Rhein-Ruhr-Zeitung. The editor-in-chief was Karl Spieker, a very able man, who had gone into exile in Canada during the Nazi period. He had been offered the post as secretary for foreign affairs in the Adenauer government, if he changed his party allegiance, but he declined the offer. When the Zentrum some years later more or less disappeared from the political map, he did join the CDU, but unfortunately, died shortly afterwards.

Personally, I am not much in favour of mixing politics and religion, but I would have preferred to see my Zentrum friends prevail with their more radical understanding of the social teaching of the Catholic Church. But the CDU had had all the advantages and the Zentrum never had a chance to catch up.

* * *

To end this chapter, want to pose a difficult question: how on earth was it possible for the Nazi regime to take over in Germany, which prides itself on its high level of culture?

When I arrived at Hagen, Westphfalia, the local head of the Kriminalpolizei (C I D), came to report to me. An elderly man with the rank of major, he stood at attention before me and declared: "Herr Sergeant! I served loyally under the Kaiser, I did the same under the Weimar republic, and under the last regime. I can assure you that I am going to serve just as faithfully under you."

He did not bat an eyelid or hesitate for a second, and he would have been most surprised if I had raised my eyebrows or even ventured to criticise him. His message was clear: "I am worthy of praise for being reliable in all circumstances." His ethos was no exception, but rather typical of the ideals of a Prussian public official. True virtue means to obey without hesitating, without reflecting on what was asked of you. The authority represented both the throne and the altar (apparently even when opposing religion). A man of duty does not question commands, he is fully at the disposal of the state. To come with objections, stemming from one's own convictions or even conscience, would be classed as disloyalty or even treason. I am afraid that it was late, too late, when the Church dared to criticise this attitude. Hitler and his regime were definitely not encouraged by the Catholic Church, but, on the other hand, it had not taught the faithful how to react against the pressure they were exposed to, and the same accusation can be made, with even more reason, against the Lutheran Church in Germany.

On the other hand, it would not be fair to compare things with the present situation. In the present Federal Republic of

Germany, Catholics make up over 50% of the population, and the episcopal conference is a factor to be reckoned with, not least economically. When Hitler came to power, Catholics were a minority in the Reich, and they had been much weakened by the Kulturkampf under Bismarck. The anti-Catholic laws were repealed as late as 1917. Catholics were thus anxious to show that they were as good patriots as anyone else, and you could hardly expect them to be among the first on the barricades to protest against the abuse of power.

I am quite convinced that the German people, with few exceptions, were not aware of how diabolical Hitler and his regime really were. They knew of persecutions of Jews and of political opponents, and that one need not protest much before being classified as an enemy of the state. They suspected that ghastly things were going on, but not the ultimate horrors, such as the systematic torture of prisoners, the methodical extermination of Jews and others in the gas chambers. I have talked to so many people in Germany, not only as a soldier, but also later, when preparing myself for religious life, and I have never met any one who had realised what things were really like in Auschwitz, Mauthausen and Bergen-Belsen.

If the warders of the camps had uttered a word about the real conditions inside, they would have been liquidated immediately. In the Swedish daily Svenska Dagbladet (22 July 1987), Mats Gellerfelt recounts two Germans, who managed to inform the Swedish and the US Foreign Office about the extermination camps, but their reports found no credence. In a biography, Harry Truman declares that it was only in April 1945 that he became aware of what was really happening. A friend of mine, a German priest, who was a soldier during the war, told me about being posted to the Neuengamme concentration camp outside Hamburg during the last year of the war. He was to instruct the personnel in air raid precaution. He had his meals with the SS in their mess, but they never mentioned by a single word what was going on inside the camp, and he was never allowed to enter it. When the war was over, the British troops took him and some other of the camp personnel to help out when Bergen-Belsen was liberated. My friend said that he just could not believe his own eyes, seeing the unspeakable misery of thousands of prisoners that looked more like skeletons than living human beings. As there was great danger of contagion, he was not allowed near them, but directed to take care of the warders, who were now to be imprisoned and tried. By chance, one of these found out that this German soldier was in fact a Catholic priest, and soon the warders lined up in order to go to confession and rid themselves of the guilt heaped upon their consciences.

This is not to be taken as an excuse for what happened, but an attempt to try to understand how it was possible. When Hitler took over in 1933, many looked upon him as a saviour from political and economic disaster. It looked like a step forward to the ordinary citizen. Simultaneously, the police state was built up and crushed all attempts at opposition with brutal efficiency. Soon, very soon, it would be too late to argue and object.

It is a great pity that more did not find the courage to refuse to cooperate, but, as I have suggested above, maybe it was difficult to stop, once you had got involved, somehow or other. Nor must we forget that the opposition got little or no support from abroad. Even Duff Cooper recalls in his memoirs, Old Men Forget, how, as a cabinet minister, he was taken to task both by colleagues and in editorials in the London Times during the last years before the war, because he had dared to criticise Hitler. In Sweden, the medical society voted against giving immigration permits to Jewish doctors, who tried to escape to Sweden from Germany. He who is without guilt may throw the first stone.

Still, having said all this, it remains unfathomable that something as ghastly as Hitler's Reich could come into existence. Too many people were prepared to accept the odious demands of the system. I do not normally drag the Devil into my arguments, but there are occasions when one just has to conclude that the mystery of Evil is a fact.

Chapter 13

Novitiate with the Jesuits

As a volunteer in the British Army, I signed on 'for the duration', i.e. until the war was over. Some months after the capitulation of Germany and Japan, those of the soldiers who had served the longest were sent home, while others had to wait their turn before being demobilized. It seemed likely that I would have to serve one more year and I started planning for the future. In December, 1945, I was given compassionate leave to visit my mother in Sweden and I used the occasion to discuss possible job openings with my father. NK, the fashionable department store in Stockholm, was willing to take me on trial in their buying department, but the salary offered was so low that it did not attract me at all.

But the commercial world was hardly included in my planning. Already in a letter to my parents (17 May 43) explaining why I wanted to join the British Army, I find the following line: "It will probably be a useful experience for me. A bit of discipline won't hurt me nor the fact that as a common soldier I shall have to live together with people of all types and learn to appreciate them." And I added: "At present, I feel that after war, I want to join a Catholic religious order and become a priest. Of course, I cannot be certain about that yet but I shall get time to think it over properly." When enlisting, I had to make a will and I left half of my small assests to the Vicar Apostolic of Sweden to help a Swede to study for the priesthood "as that is what I wanted to be myself".

During my time as a soldier, I used several short leaves to visit monasteries in order to get personal experience of what religious life could be like. I made a retreat with the

Jesuits at Osterley, London; spent a weekend in Ampleforth Abbey, Yorkshire, and a week in Prinknash Abbey outside Gloucester, both belonging to the Benedictine Order but quite different from each other in character. At Ampleforth I got the impression that life there was centred around the boarding school, for which it is renowned. Prinknash was more to my taste. The monks had originally been Anglicans but they moved more and more towards the Roman Catholic Church until the whole community changed allegiance. Their life style was more truly Benedictine, as I saw it, with Matins at a very early hour and a day characterized by St. Benedict's motto Ora et labora, work and pray. All the monks helped out in running the farm, repairing the buildings and other menial duties. Belonging to another branch of the Benedictine family, they always stayed in their monastery and had neither schools nor parishes.

The guestmaster at Prinknash was Dom Bede Griffith, later to become well-known both through his autobiography and by going to India, where he founded an Ashram. He struck me as being both intellectually sharp and very spiritual. I felt really at home at Prinknash, so much so that I talked to the abbot, Dom Wilfred Upsom, about becoming a priest. He told me that it was not unlikely that I had a vocation, but added: "Just because you have liked it so much here at Prinknash, don't leave us thinking that this is the only possible place for you to serve the Lord." Not every abbot gives such wise and altruistic advice.

Serving as a soldier in Europe, I met many priests and saw a great variety of religious institutions. I became more and more convinced that I should study for priesthood in a religious order. While on leave in Sweden at the end of 1945, I visited Uppsala and the Jesuit Fr. Josef Gerlach for whom I had a message. One of his brothers had been interned in the Dachau concentration camp but died shortly after being liberated by the Allied forces. A friend of mine, a German priest who had also been in Dachau, asked me to pass on this information to Fr. Gerlach, as Germans at this time were not allowed to write letters abroad.

I used the opportunity to talk with Fr. Gerlach about my future. He stressed the importance of having Swedish priests working in their native country. If I wanted to do so as a member of a religious order, there were two alternatives at the time: the German Jesuits and the French Dominicans. Without hesitation, I opted for the Jesuits. If I had become a Catholic, I might as well go the whole hog and join the Jesuits, whose machinations every young Swede had learnt to abhor.

I had positive motives also. The first Jesuit I had met was Fr. John LaFarge, a gifted and versatile priest, who was a forerunner in the field of racial and social justice as well as in liturgical renewal. He was the spiritual director of St. Ansgar's American Scandinavian Catholic League in New York and he had made a deep impression on me. By the way, Sigrid Undset, the Nobel prize winner, was also a member of the League, but I am afraid I had not read any of her books at that stage and failed to appreciate the honour of meeting her. Once, she was to give a talk on the Norse sagas but was indisposed so Fr. LaFarge read her manuscript. Every now and then he looked up and started quoting by heart the old Icelandic text, one of the many languages he had mastered. Yet he was both humble and unsophisticated, as the title of his autobiography suggests: The Manner is Ordinary (a quotation from the Jesuit rule).

When I returned to Germany I went to Cologne to see the Jesuit provincial whose jurisdiction included Scandinavia. I was called to interviews with four priests and was accepted as a postulant in the Society of Jesus (the official name of the Jesuit order). Before I could join I had to wait for demobilization and permission to stay in Germany.

* * *

Before taking the final step, one important thing remained: to tell my mother about it. Before leaving Sweden to go to the USA, I had promised to come back. Now five years had passed instead of the one originally planned. I was the only one of her children to live with her after the divorce, and she had envisaged a future where I married and provided her with several grandchildren. Instead of this rosy picture, I was going to spend many more years away from her, and as a Jesuit and a priest renounce the possibility of having a family. Some years later, staying at the Brigittine sisters' hospice in Lugano, she met a US Catholic couple who expressed their envy that her son was studying for priesthood. But my mother replied: "God stole my son." Well, I can imagine Catholic mothers having the same reaction.

I wrote a letter to her explaining my intentions. I cannot remember the contents of it any longer, and in spite of the fact that my mother kept many letters from this period, I have found no trace of it. Maybe she tore it up, hoping to rid herself of it all that way. Before my papers came through, I invited my mother to England. We stayed with relatives and went for long walks while discussing my decision. She could not understand me, yet she did not try to make me change my mind. It must have been difficult for her in more than one way, listening to my standpoints, so strange to her, and having to "talk religion", something she had hardly ever done before. But occasionally, she would come in like a flash. She explained that she could not recite the Our Father "because you say: 'Forgive us our sins, as we forgive those who sin against us.' There are things that I cannot forgive." She was too honest to just slide over those words.

While waiting for my papers, I had already visited the novitiate at Eringerfeld, near Lippstadt, and left most of my belongings there. On November, 25, 1946, I was driven from my army quarters in Dortmund to Arnsberg. At 1100 hours, I received a paper stating that I was demobilized and authorized to reside in Germany. At 1230 hours the military vehicle rolled across the drawbridge of Eringerfeld and I got out. Though still in uniform, I was a civilian and could start my novitiate.

* * *

"Eringerfeld is an old hunting castle from 1648 with four towers and a moat, though it is now without water. There are four large halls. One is used as a refectory, another as recreation room. The rest have been split up and are used, together with several smaller rooms, as dormitories and studies for the novices. 5 — 6 novices share a dormitory. Altogether there are close to 60 persons in the house, 7 priests, 41 novices and 7 lay brothers as well as two novices who intend to become brothers.

To the north of the castle there is a spacious park surrounded by a forest and arable and pasture land." That is the way my father described the novitiate in a circular letter

to the family, having visited it in June 1948. And he added:
"Just now (7 a.m.) several novices are leaving the house,
some in their black habits to walk in the peaceful park,
meditating or reciting their prayers. Others rush by with
rolled-up sleeves, slacks and track shoes to go for a run.

I study the boys. Some of them seem happy and ready for
a joke, others are serene and contemplative. A few of them
appear to be rather highly-strung, perhaps trying to imitate
Ignatius of Loyola."

It is a pity that no one could explain to my father that
those who overdid it and tried to become saints straight
away usually left the novitiate. You cannot force God's
hand that way.

I was entering a new world in more than one way. The life
of ease and plenty that the soldiers of the army of occupation
enjoyed was gone. We had lived in real luxury, at least in
comparison with the average German. They were short of
almost everything. If they found anything to buy, the owner
did not want to exchange it for cash, but demanded goods
or precious objects. Everyone knew that a devaluation was
due as too many Reichsmarks had been issued. As it was,
it took two years before the authorities got around to it.
Afterwards we received only a few D-marks so that for a
while, we could not afford to buy stamps for more than one
letter a month.

As a soldier, I had been given more than enough to eat
and there was great variety of food. Now our day started
with a watery gruel and for the main meals, there was a
constant fare of potatoes mixed with nettles. Not the tender
early-season nettles that we had used at home to make a
delicious soup, but tall, stinging ones which we gathered
in the moat. For dessert, there was always rhubarb which
had grown tall and become stringy. It was prepared with
artificial sweetening, sugar being non-existent. We hardly
ever saw meat and there was no cooking fat or butter. Tea
and coffee were made from substitutes. To begin with, I
was scandalized to see the huge quantities that the novices
put away, but soon I behaved the same myself. "Lars has
an incredible appetite" my father commented in the letter
quoted above.

This probably sounds as if it had been a cultural shock

to me, and of course it was. But it did not worry me in the least. This was where I wanted to be and nothing could dampen the joy I felt at being in the novitiate. St. Theresa of Lisieux once said that when you are in love, you tend to do a lot of foolish things. I was prepared for any follies that the Lord might have in store for me. The Catholic students in Uppsala later wrote some satirical verses about the novitiate being a home, where they skin you to the bone. But I did not need any black humour to keep going though of course it was tough at times.

In his letter, my father had described our novice master as "a cheerful and pleasant man of 40, who had been an orderly in the German medical corps right through the war". That was true, but the soldier's life had hardly touched him. He had the ambition to form his novices with the help of the great masters of the spiritual life, but his previous knowledge of them was scant. Trying to make up for it, he taxed himself too much and maybe us too. He had a rather narrow view of how a young Jesuit should behave. If a novice did not conform, he would incur the novice master's displeasure. It was a pity because in that way, some gifted people were unnecessarily restrained in their development or even had to leave the Society.

Our day started at 5.30 a.m. and before breakfast, we had had an hour's meditation and Mass and Communion. The rest of the morning was devoted to spiritual reading, studies of Latin and the rules and history of the Jesuit order. There were also various chores to be done in the house or the garden, all neatly divided into periods from quarter of an hour up to one hour. During meals, someone read aloud, first from Scripture, then a book of history (during holidays it could be replaced by lighter reading). After the siesta we had more lectures, studies or time for prayer until supper. After a free period, we gathered to listen to "points" for the morning's meditation and lights-out was around 9.30 p.m.

During the day we kept silence, with the exception of a recreation period after meals, when we went for a walk in groups of three according to a list, which was changed every week. We were thus to learn to mix with everybody. Necessary conversation during the day was to be kept short

which came easy as we were supposed to talk in Latin only,
or should I say dog-Latin

Thursday was a free day which meant that we went for
a long walk in the morning and had the afternoon off. On
Sundays there were no lectures and we had time to write
home, go for a private walk or indulge in reading. The
owner of the castle gave us permission to gather firewood
from the forest so novices could often be seen going off
into the woods with an axe or a saw. Such breaks in the
ordinary routine were highly appreciated. In spite of the
firewood, we felt the cold. There was no way to heat our
dormitories and more than once, we found a thin layer of
ice on the water of the washbasin in the morning. During
my first winter at Eringerfeld, the novices spent most of the
day packed together in the "tower room" with a tiny stove
in the far corner. The air was thick and sitting there shoulder
to shoulder, reading, studying, meditating, we really felt
the lack of Lebensraum or elbow room. It could set the
nerves jangling but fortunately the novice master showed
understanding for such reactions. When it hit you badly,
he let you sleep a bit longer in the morning or sent you out
for a walk on your own.

A visit to the dentist meant a six mile walk to Geseke. If
someone sent me a gift parcel of cooking fat and meat from
abroad, I had to walk ten miles to Lippstadt to pick it up.
Later on, we acquired a moped and I was allowed to do
errands with it, another welcome change from the routine.

* * *

The most important part of the novitiate was the long retreat,
or the spiritual exercises of St. Ignatius. Under the direction
of the novice master we spent four weeks meditating on God
and his creation; the rebellion of sin and God's answer to
it, the Incarnation; the life of Christ and his gospel; the
passion of Christ and finally his resurrection and ascension.
The exercises end with a contemplation of God's goodness
as evidenced in Christ and in the beauty of the whole of
creation.

In his annotations to the Spiritual Exercises, St. Ignatius
stresses that it is not knowing much that gives satisfaction
to the soul but seeing and tasting things from within. The
retreat master must not unduly influence the participants. It

is desirable that 'the Creator and Lord himself can communicate with the pious person in search of the will of God'.

These four weeks of meditation and contemplative prayer made an enormous inpact on me. In my first letter home afterwards I find the following comment: "By and by, we are returning to the normal routine — unfortunately, because in the silent peace, protected against all disturbing elements, we found paths towards undiscovered regions." And towards the end of the letter, I asked my mother's pardon if I had bubbled over with enthusiasm but I hoped that she would understand my need to let others participate in all the gifts that had been heaped upon me.

It was a pity that it was not until later that I found the following passage in a book by the Swedish author Harry Martinson. It would have been a good illustration for my mother:

"No truths remains in you as naturally as those found in silence. Everything talks. Sun and grass and flowers, lakes, people who pass by or come towards you. And anyone who does not start thinking has only himself to blame. In silence, there is room for everything at the same time; whereas when you talk, there is but room for one thing at a time."

The joy that filled me after these spiritual exercises tended to overflow. I did not regret my choice of life, but I felt that being a Jesuit was not enough. Their life was too worldly, spending much of their times on other things than prayer. So I told the novice master that I would probably have to leave the novitiate to join another, more contemplative order, either the Trappists or the Carthusians. He was convinced — quite rightly — that I was not suited for such a life, but he found it difficult to convince me. In the end, he asked the rector of the house to talk to me, an old and experienced priest, but a bit rough in his ways. "What, do you want to spend half the day singing the office? Who could stick that? Do you expect to think only of God the whole day long? It would drive you crazy, I know from my experience visiting such monasteries."

I thought his answer sounded stupid, but I came out of his room cured. I did want to be a Jesuit, after all.

It is useful to be confronted occasionally with blunt statements. At Prinknash Abbey, I had found it easy to pray and

I talked to the abbot about my spiritual experiences. I had
difficulties in fitting them into the pattern that I had read
about in St John of the Cross. It was not like The Ascent
of Mount Carmel, nor The Dark Night of The Soul. The
last stage, The Living Flame of Love, seemed more apt to
describe my experiences. Whereupon the abbot smiled and
said: "My dear boy, what makes you think that you are
anywhere near the first stage?"

* * *

The two years of novitiate came to an end. To outsiders,
it might appear to be a long period. I found that it had
passed very quickly and I never had any regrets about my
choice. Towards the end, I had been spending more time
studying Latin, having had none at school, and needing it
badly as it was the main language used in seminary teaching
at the time.

The only time that the outside world disturbed our secluded
life was in the middle of 1947. The old rector called me in
and told me that according to rumours, the Russians were
preparing to move westwards. Could I as a former British
soldier get help from the Army to evacuate the novitiate
and send all of us into safety across the Rhine? I was not
to mention a word of all this to the other novices, however.
I remember waking up at night and I could hear columns of
tanks driving along the B 1, the main road from Berlin to
Cologne, which ran a few miles north of us. So the Russians
have started to move, I thought, and felt very uneasy, until I
realized what the noise really was. The wind came from the
north and carried the sound of limestone being crushed in
a cement factory.

Still, the idea of a confrontation with Russia was no
great surprise. The coalition between the western powers and
Communism was not a natural one, but war makes strange
bed-fellows. At the time of Stalingrad, the Russians and
Stalin had been crowned with wreaths of glory, which had
soon started to wilt. Shortly after the armistice, we started
hearing about people having been abducted and taken to the
Russian zone. As a soldier in Iserlohn, I had to follow up a
report that a person had been kidnapped in plain daylight in
the very centre of town. That involved going to the nearest
Russian military mission to make an official protest. We got

only smiles and denials as an answer but I felt decidedly uneasy while inside their confines.

Criticism of the Russians became more common and rumours were spread. As a sergeant, I had to send in a weekly report on our activities. The length of the report tended to be in inverse ratio to the amount of work accomplished. One week I had done practically nothing, so I sat down and wrote a P.M. entitled Moscow Gold. It was all about infiltration from the East, Russian money for political parties etc, etc. Everything was built on rumours and I did not have a single fact to adduce, but the ground was apparently prepared for it. My text was reprinted in monthly reports all the way up to the SHAEF Bulletin (Supreme Head Quarters of the Allied Expeditionary Force in Europe). Cracks had already appeared in the accord reached in the conferences of Yalta and Potsdam and the cold war was overtaking us.

* * *

After the novitiate, I was sent to the Juniorate, a year of classical and humanistic studies. The accent was on Latin and Greek but we also read the history of literature and culture. The priest in charge, Fr. Wilhelm Bönner, was so full of vigour, in spite of his age, that we nicknamed him Father Vitalis. During the 1930's he had been member of a team of Jesuits who travelled round Germany trying to counteract the Nazi ideology. When the powers that be stopped their activities, he went to a Jesuit college in Cairo to be out of their reach. Before World War I, he had spent a few years teaching in the Jesuit school outside Copenhagen and he understood that a lone Swede could sometimes feel a bit out of water in German surroundings.

Our juniorate was located in Pullach outside Munich in "a modern and practical building on the main road to Innsbruck. From my room on the top floor, I have an inspiring view of the Alps. Life is more varied here than in the novitiate. There are some 150 Jesuits in the house from all parts of Germany and Austrians, Hungarians, Slovenes, Lithuanians, Swiss and Frenchmen, which widens the perspective and helps me to understand that there are various ways of being a Jesuit. I learn to distinguish between local customs and the universal traits" (27 Aug 48).

Our Latin teacher was Fr. Rump, who had spent all

his active life in Jesuit schools. He treated us rather like first formers but we made quick progress in our studies. Fr. Rump made quite an impression on me. Well over 80, and with three heart attacks behind him, he kept on unperturbed. When reading the letters of Cicero we ran into the term 'Stoics'. Who were they, he asked, and got the correct answer:"Philosophers." And what did they teach? — "To fight your passions until you finally arrived at 'apatheia', a balance, or even, you might say, indifference." — Correct again. Now is that a good philosophy?

The young and very innocent Jesuit sugggested that this was a short but good summary of the Christian ascetical ideal, which made old Fr. Rump explode. He pulled himself up in the chair, banged the table three times with his clenched fists and said: "No, no, no! It is a bad philosophy, about the worst imaginable. You must not stifle your passions. They are your driving forces. You should learn to control them and steer them properly, not kill them. If you eradicate them, you will never achieve anything in life." Fr. Rump and Fr. Bönner taught me much about the positive outlook on man which is typical of a genuine Jesuit. I also learnt a lot of Latin that year, much more than I would have during four years of secondary school in Sweden. We treated Latin as a living language and used it in everyday life and conversation. They did not limit our reading to the 'golden age' of Cicero, Ceasar and Livius. We read the Vulgate version of the Bible and various stories written in vivid medieval Latin, which we were encouraged to imitate. Our tests included writing short essays in Latin without the help of a dictionary or a grammar.

I found Greek much more difficult, being the only one in class who had not read a word of it at school (I had picked up the alphabet and the first steps of the grammar during the last months in the novitiate.) With the help of a good teacher, however, I got enough to continue on my own and was later able to read both the New Testament and some texts of the Greek Fathers. But Homer's Iliad was definitely beyond me.

As a Scandinavian, I was given the task of presenting Sigrid Undset's famous novel Kristin Lavransdatter to the class. I was completely fascinated by it — "the book grips me so that I would rather continue reading and do nothing else until I have finished the three volumes", I state in a letter home (17 Jan 49). But that was not possible. Our daily routine included meditation, Mass and several lectures, but I kept on reading until I could not keep my eyes open any longer, with one exception. In chapter four of the second volume, Kristin is expecting her first child. She has been in labour for ten days with much physical pain but also suffered qualms of conscience. The child had been conceived before she was properly wedded and she was convinced that God would punish her with a deformed child.

When I had finished the chapter I was quite exhausted and had to lie down and rest. It was as if I had gone through labour pains myself, so vivid is Sigrid Undset's writing. I now regretted that I had not read her much earlier and had missed the chance of getting to know her personally when we met in New York.

* * *

Nowadays, a young Jesuit would look upon the life style of our juniorate as something really oldfashioned and strict, but to us, it was very open, compared with the novitiate. We shared much of our day with the students of the school of philosophy. At times, we got together and produced shows with music borrowed from operas and operettas but with new texts in which we joked about the professors and the routine of our daily life. We made excursions, always on foot, and once I was deceived into going for a walk which involved 20 miles there and 20 miles back. We did not have any pocket money, not even to buy a beer or a cup of coffee. I got such blisters under my feet that I was obliged to use felt slippers for a whole week.

Others climbed the Alps, got caught in a snowstorm and had to bivouac up there, arriving back home the following day, which was definitely frowned upon, not least by the professor who was prefect for the students. He was too zealous and new restrictive rules appeared almost daily on the bulletin board. But we had learnt not to take it all lying down and reacted with various pranks. One day someone had even produced a small capsule with tear gas, which was hidden in the napkin of the said professor. It did not take long before he left the refectory in tears and many others were similarly affected. The rector suggested that this time we had gone too far.

* * *

My superiors had decided that after the humanistic studies, I was to spend two years studying philosphy instead of the normal three. It was a sensible decision as I needed the classical studies but was a few years older than most of my classmates. I especially appreciated the fact that I was to go to England for philosophy. The climate of Munich includes the Föhn, a warm alpine wind which did not suit me at all — "it gives me headaches and makes me feel very weary" (17 Jan 49). Furthermore, I had got a glimpse of the way they studied philosophy in Pullach and it was definitely not my style. Kant was a shining light and they got involved in deep and complicated arguments which seemed too rationalistic to me. I had come to the conclusion that if I had to do my philosophy there, I would lose both my faith and my reason. As it was, I could keep both and at the same time return to England, where I knew that I would feel at home.

Chapter 14

Philosophical and Theological Studies in England

Having spent two summers in England before the war, three years in the USA and over three years as a soldier in the British Army, the Anglo-Saxon world had become almost as familiar to me as my native Sweden.

While in Germany, I had established good relations with my Jesuit brethren. As a soldier I had made the acquaintance of many Germans and some of them had become my close friends. At first, the members of the Occupation Forces were not supposed to have any personal contacts with Germans. It was not a good rule, perpetuating as it did the dislike or even hate without which people are not willing to go to war and kill those on the other side. Furthermore, the BBC having given the Germans the impression that the Allied forces came as liberators if not friends, it was hardly reasonably to tell the soldiers to treat them as dust. The rule could easily stimulate unfair treatment of the conquered and encourage various forms of private confiscations (which were of course nothing in comparison with the official looting that had gone on the 'good old days', when it was seen as a way of paying off the mercenaries. We like to imagine that we are more civilized and humane nowadays, even in warfare).

The non-fraternization rule was fortunately soon lifted. It had never applied to us in the Field Security. On the contrary, we were supposed to cultivate German acquaintances in order to carry out our duties. I had come to know many priests and politicians, but my closest friend was Rudi Hesse in Iserlohn. We met in the early days of the occupation outside a church and I offered him a proper cigarette (unavailable to Germans at the time). This led to a lasting friendship which came to include relatives on both sides so that I even refer to Iserlohn as my German home town.

* * *

Before continuing my studies I spent the summer vacation in Sweden. It gave me a chance to get to know my Jesuit brethren there and the situation of Catholics in my own country. But most important of all was seeing my family again, especially my mother. I tried to help her understand that she had not lost me when I became a Catholic and a Jesuit. Looking through our correspondence before and after that summer, I notice a difference: I preach less to her and she seems to have come out of her defensive attitude against my decisions in life. Our relationship had returned to normal.

* * *

The seminary training of a Jesuit comprised three years of philosophical and four years of theological studies. I was to spend only two year on philosophy but it still added up to a lot of studying. The English Jesuits had their own place of studies Heythrop College, a former manor halfway between Oxford and Stratford. Two wings had been added to the imposing main building, one housing the philosophers, the other the theologians. "My room is large and airy, that is draughty, as is often the case in this country. But it has central heating which they say works quite well. Let's see if that is true" I wrote in my first report home. My scepticism was not unfounded. I have vivid memories of getting frostbite every winter.

The estate was extensive and included a cricket ground, a football ground and even a golf course. During the afternoon break we students worked maintaining the large gardens. To us the most important feature of the garden were the huts, where we made tea and sometimes cooked meals. The professors liked to be invited and we had very friendly relations with them. We could knock on their doors almost any time to discuss questions relating to our studies. The director of studies tried to keep the number of lectures down and let the individual decide the pace of studies, 'the very opposite to Pullach' was my comment in the same letter. I had profited from my classical studies for I could add that 'today we had our first lectures, one of which was entirely in Latin, and I had no trouble following it'.

I estimate that during my Jesuit training I attended some

5,000 lectures, all of them obligatory. Consequently, it is impossible to attempt to summarize the various subjects taught, the very titles of which sound exotic: epistomology, ontology, theodicy, fundamental theology, eschatology, patristics. Many of them were interesting and much of what we learned was of value later on in life.

In a letter home towards the end of the first term, I state that "I like philosophy" and I continued to do so throughout the course. We tackled fundamental questions of philosophy and looked at them from various points of view. In epistomology we asked ourselves how man can obtain true knowledge. We studied the theory of science psychology and logic. In metaphysics we asked intricate questions about being in itself — das Ding an sich — and its presuppositions. This led us on to the question whether man, relying on his natural gifts of insight and reasoning, can arrive at any true knowledge of God.

All this might sound complicated, and it was. It probably also sounds like the kind of thing that monks used to speculate about and that is quite correct. Every student had a portable set of the standard works of St. Thomas Aquinas, Summa Theologica and Summa Contra Gentiles. The professors often referred to them (in spite of their titles, both works deal mainly with philosophical problems). According to taste and interest we could delve further into these and other books of thomistic philosophy. It originated with the Dominican Thomas Aquinas who in the 13th century tried to make a synthesis between the realistic approach to philosophy of Aristotle and the more idealistic line of Platonism, which had had great influence in the history of the early church.

Even though 700 years had passed since St. Thomas himself had lectured at Paris his views were held in great esteem by our professors. That does not mean that they were repeated in a petrified form. During the centuries, his basic concepts have been confronted with and modified by other philosphical trends. The nominalism of the late Middle Ages tended to undermine the very basis of realistic philopsophy in a way that explains much of the upheaval during the passage from medieval to modern times in the religious as well as the secular sphere of thought. Thomism almost disappeared from the map until it was revived in the Catholic Church in the first half of the 19th cent. In the early 1950's there was a period of renewal with thinkers like Maréochal using a thomistic approach to try to solve the fundamental problems of the theory of knowledge raised by the kantian school of philosophy.

Many thomists have rendered their master a disservice by maintaining that a ready answer to every problem is found in his works. That is obviously not the case. I would rather suggest that his special claim to fame was his ability to pose questions and delineate problems with startling clarity.

Another typical trait of Thomas is his realism. He was a disciple of Albertus Magnus, author of several books on natural science, and for Aristotle, the inspirer of Thomas, observation of natural phenomena was the starting point of philosophy. In spite of all his speculation and acumen, Thomas Aquinas was not a rationalist but had his feet firmly planted in reality (though to him this was not synonymous with palpable and measurable quantity). When he talks of "possibilities" they always had an intrinsic relation to reality, i.e. they had existed or would exist in the future. Not all scholastic philosophers had the same solid basis for their concepts. Suarez (who had some followers among my professors at Heythrop College) held that everything was "possible" that could exist. A thinker like Occam (whose influence was great in the late medieval period) went further and his chapter De possibilibus — on what is possible — is quite impossible even to read.

I soon found out that there was quite a range of opinion on philosophical problems among our professors and we could widen that range by using the large library placed at our disposition, which included almost every trend of thought, both modern and ancient. Great emphasis was laid on the history of philosophy and we were fortunate in having a distinguished professor, Fr. F.C. Copleston, as our teacher. He had became well-known for his BBC discussions with Bertrand Russell and others, for a Penguin book on Thomas Aquinas and as a guest lecturer in many countries. Fr. Copleston was a prolific author as is evident by his nine volume History of Philosophy, which he wrote entirely on his own, an unusual feat. It has rightly become a standard work and is as readable and enjoyable as were his lectures. Books on the history of philosophy often evaluate the various philosophers from the writer's own point of view. Fr. Copleston tries to present every philosopher as fairly as possible, describing his background, how he came to develop his thoughts and his influence on later generations. Towards the end he gently asks to what extent the philosopher in question managed to solve the problems posed and points out difficulties that might arise from the way he solved them.

* * *

In an attempt at systematic studies of the basic problems of philosophy, we tried to reflect on both our own thoughts and those proposed by 'real' philosophers. Our professors presented their subject matter in the form of propositions, rather like those supposedly nailed to the church door by Luther, but it was just the heading that sounded like a dry, crisp statement. There was a standard way of presenting their matter. First came the status questionis, putting the question into its historical context. Then ample time was spent on explaining the meaning of the terminology involved. We realized the importance of grasping exactly what was meant by every single word enounced in the proposition and became aware of the fact that often differences of opinion are due to words rather than thoughts: we use the same words but refer to different things by them. The professor then made a survey of those opposing his proposition, giving their views and the reasons for them. Having gone through all this, a proof of the truth contained in the proposition was proffered, but by then we had already become familiar with most of the arguments in favour of it.

In our exercises we still used the medieval form of dis-putation in the so-called syllogistic form. Let me give an example:
Major: Darwin's theory of evolution is contrary to the biblical account in Genesis (First book of Moses).
Minor: But everything in the Bible is true.
Conclusion: Therefore the theory of evolution is not true.

It was customary to have a major on which both could agree. The opponent did not accept the conclusion but he usually attacked the minor. Either he denied its validity completely, whereupon the respondent had to prove it, showing

his presuppositions, and it became obvious that the difference of opinion was of a more fundamental character
and that had to be cleared up before you could argue the
particular case. This more or less equates to the method of
asking 'why? 'and demanding an answer, called the socratic
method after its originator, Socrates.

But the respondent had another option. He could reflect
on his own line of reasoning and try to find the point
of divergence. In that case he would say: Distinguo —
I distinguish between your way of putting it and mine.
Getting back to our example about Darwin and the Bible,
he would say:

How are we to understand the word "true"? I agree that
Scripture is true, seen as a message from God. But its aim
is to enrich our views on religion, not to give us accurate
scientific information. I therefore reject your conclusion.

It is now up to the respondent to prove that his use of
the word "true" is correct, and so the disputation goes on
until they agree or one of them gives up, not finding any
further valid arguments to fall back on. The syllogistic form
of disputation is something of a straight-jacket which suits
some but not others and it can admittedly degenerate into
a kind of intellectual steeplechase. But used in the correct
way it helps the individual to become more aware of what
he is talking about it. Furthermore, by revealing the basis
on which we found our arguments it forces both sides to
get down to fundamentals.

Very often we are not conscious of our own presuppositions — or those of others — unless they are brought out into
the open. In the example I used we forget that the Genesis
version of creation was composed at a time when everybody,
including the scientists, had a completely different picture of
the universe. The earth was flat, there was water above the
sky and below the earth (to explain rain and rivers). The sun
and the moon were drawn on heavenly carriages across the
sky, which is placed above the earth like a cheese-cover. And
so forth. No one thought of questioning these views, nor
could they imagine that the text of Genesis would one day
be read by people with quite different views on the structure
of the universe.

We on the other hand use modern science as a basis

for our criticism of the Genesis story but miss the main point that the author wanted to make, namely that there is only one God and creator behind everything, instead of the common view that there are myriads of deities behind the various manifestations in life. We consider ourselves modern and enlightened when we refer to the Big-Bang theory, but forget to put the question that immediately suggests itself: "What was is it that exploded in the Big Bang? Where did it come from? And how does the result of it all happen to be so differentiated and well designed?"

All too easily we sweep various questions under the carpet or do not even pose them. It is especially important to query our basic attitudes when faced with situations where we react emotionally. Start out by asking almost banal questions: why do I support Arsenal rather than Tottenham (or the Giants instead of the Dodgers)? Move on to other fields such as my reaction towards people from various parts of the country, foreigners, races, political or religious groups. The inquiry can become an interesting journey, revealing things about myself that I had never imagined. It is by no means easy to be uncompromisingly tolerant towards others, or towards oneself. There is a saying about skeletons in the cupboard and most people prefer to keep the door shut on them. That is human, but it does not make you more human if you behave in this way.

Freud talked about repressions, tranference and sublimation. It is undoubtedly important to bring things out of the unconscious in order to starting dealing with them in the open. Our subconsious is filled with experiences which we might not even remember, but some of them we have relegated there knowingly, in order not to have to face up to them. Consequently, not all our diffuse feelings of guilt are without basis — they might have a background history of bad conscience. If anyone happens to allude to such things, it will call forth violent reactions in us, unless we are willing to confront the ethical decision anew.

* * *

In order to function properly as a human being one needs to stand on firm ground. The philosophers have a major problem: how am I able to know anything for certain? I was brought up in a Sweden where people preferred to avoid the question Kant and his followers have left an indelible impressions on our way of thinking. In the 1950's a Lutheran bishop declared that the kantian critic of the human mind 'made me into a liberal theologian. If I had been able to overcome these philosophical problems and become say a thomist, my theological views would have changed profoundly'. Faced with the discussion regarding faith and reason, a Protestant university chaplain stated that people who demanded to know about God had not understood the very point of religion.

But was my faith then a blind leap into the unknown — and unknowable? Had I thrown myself into the arms of someone who, according to common opinion, did not exist or about whom I could have no knowledge? I found this an absurd way of thinking. It could be compared to the liberal theologians who admitted that it was possible that Jesus had never existed but 'the important thing is to believe in him'.

If there is no bridge between faith and reason, there can be no faith, and no one to believe in. And if man cannot know anything for certain, what is left? I refused to accept the way that Kant and his followers had disintegrated the world we live in. How can I start discussing with someone without first accepting as a fact that both of us exist in a surrounding world. Otherwise I fall into the dilemma of the solipsist, whose philosophy taught him that he exists, but nothing else. "My only difficulty is how to convince others that this is the only true philosophy."

Surely I become aware of myself only in confrontation with the outside world. The consciousness of a child grows through the stimulations it receives. I wake up to a new day when the alarm clock rings or when the sunlight penetrates my eyelids. A human being develops his intrinsic qualities meeting other persons, talking to them and learning from them. Romulus and Remus were lucky having each other. In modern days, when children have been discovered in the forest, having been brought up by animals, they turned out to be underdeveloped due to lack of contact with other human beings.

Philosophising about knowledge and about being has to

start somewhere, and that somewhere cannot be a critical
vacuum. Ex nihilo nihil is an axiom in scholastic philosophy
— from nothing comes nothing. I can never prove my own
existence from the outside. If I try to do so, I am begging
the question.

Apart from the fact that it would be most inconvenient
to suppose that nothing really exists, it turns out to be
an illogical statement. It's rather like the problem of free
will. If you treat it exclusively as a theoretical problem, it is
difficult to handle. But accept it as a fact and it can become
the starting point of a philosphical analysis. Chesterton loved
tangible reasons and when he met someone who refused to
accept free will he told them: "I am going to start hitting
you, and I shall stop only when you admit that I can if I
will." Chesterton being a big and hefty man, it was a
weighty argument.

In the same way, it is necessary to find a starting point for
the problem of knowledge, where reality and our reflection
over it meet (or where the logical and ontological planes
intersect, as a scholastic philosopher would put it).

I found a book written by a professor at Louvain, Louis
de Raymaeker, which suited me perfectly: Saisie de L'Etre,
which means to grasp, get a hold on reality (or being). It
is necessary to begin with an experience which is concrete
and intellectual at the same time, an intuition which makes
you see, both literally and mentally, what it means to be, to
exist. It is not by placing yourself in a void or vacuum that
you achieve this, on the contrary, it has to be a vivid human
experience of reality.

I had had such an experience myself up on Le Reculet in
the French Jura mountains when all the alps were piled up in
front of me. How intensely aware I had become at that time,
both of my own existence and of that of the surrounding
world! And the world around me had become transparent
and made me think of the hymn We thank Thee God for
this fair earth. I would overreach myself if I were to suggest
that every sound philosophy immediately leads to God. But
my experience had given me a good foothold which could
be the starting point for a realistic philosophy. I studied De
Raymaeker's book through and through and I often refer to
it as 'my philosophical bible'. After all, I had found a man

who had reflected deeply about things that I had personally experienced.

* * *

During two years we tackled most of the problems of philosophy and studied various attempts to solve them. Having passed our final exam we felt that 'now we should really start studying philosophy'. But by then it was time to move on to theology. It had been a good exercise for our reasoning power and simultaneously given us an insight into the way people had struggled with the problems posed by the human condition. Having a more thorough knowledge of different ways of thinking might later help us in our pastoral work. I enjoyed studying philosophy but I do not think that I would like to devote myself full-time to the subject. I do have a good deal of confidence in the human power of reasoning but one must not exaggerate it or think that we can build theoretical systems that solve all problems. And I definitely would not like to spend my time following up the type of philosophical criticism which tries to punch holes in everything or the logical positivism which hides reality from us the way the Potemkin village did.

We now passed on to theology to deepen our faith and our understanding of it. We read the Old and the New Testament, looked at the historical context in which they had been conceived and written and delved into text criticism. In patristics we read the Greek as well as the Latin fathers to see how they transmitted the message of Christ and to find out where they put their accents, both as far as the content and the structure of the Church was concerned. We studied church history and saw how the councils from Nicea (325 A.D.) onwards attempted to assimilate the fulness of revelation and find ways to formulate it so as to safeguard essential truths.

This stood us in good stead when we came to dogmatic theology which is important for a Catholic. We read systematic treatises on Christ, the Church, grace, the seven sacraments, and eschatology or the last things. We were supposed to study not only facts but also follow the development and living tradition of the Church and learn to interpret its dogmatic statements against the background of the discussions that had preceded it and the schisms it had caused. We studied the way various theologians had tried to understand the contents of their faith in the light of the world they lived in. The kernel of our Christian faith is found in divine revelation but it has been given to us as human beings and we are to reflect over it. The talent must not be buried in the ground but used so that we can profit from it.

Let me give an example of the interaction between faith and reason. What is conscience? In psychology, we found that man through his rational insight has the possibility of choosing and making decisions. Ethics dealt with norms of behaviour and maintained that we "ought" to follow them. Conscience is a gauge indicating to what extent we follow our ethical insight and put it into practice. I have for instance been taught that "thou shalt not steal". If I look at something attractive that belongs to someone else, I get a bad conscience if I start giving in to temptation, but a good conscience if I resist and try to live up to the norm.

This analysis is limited to normal human reasoning. In moral theology, we went further and asked questions about norms: is it always right to keep to them, are they in conformity with the Christian faith and teaching? We must not follow civil laws and commands blindly and uncritically. It is more important to obey God than man. If our conscience tells us it is wrong, we are not excused by saying that it is permitted by or prescribed in civil law.

For a Christian, conscience is not only a human gauge to indicate how we put our ethical norms into practice. It is also the place where God intervenes in our lives. It is here that we are to work out our salvation by being sensitive to the promptings of the Holy Spirit. But conscience can also be a place of momentous consequences if we try to go against it and shut God out of our lives. The text "whatsoever you have done to the least of my brethren, you have done to me" is immediately followed by its opposite: "What you have not done to him, you have not done to me either."

At the same time, it is here that we find an answer to the burning question of the fate of those who are not Christians. There were times when theologians suggested that outside the visible church, there could be no salvation. That cannot be true, if you consider that every one is responsible for the way he decides in his conscience, according to the norm given to him. In baptism and other sacraments, God promises to give us special gifts but that does not mean that his hands are bound. He can and surely does give his grace to whom he wants and how he wants. The Spirit is present in every conscience and this is the place where man decides for or against God. No one can claim exclusive rights to the gifts of God and has even less reason to believe that these will be of avail to him if he does not follow his conscience and the promptings of the Holy Spirit. And no one needs to feel neglected or abandoned because in the anonymity of his inner man, he meets his Creator. There he can decide for Him and receive his gifts, without there being any need to put labels on the gifts or on the recipient of them.

* * *

It feels like cheating to stop my acount here but my intention is to give a glimpse into what happened during the six years of my studies, not to write a handbook on Catholic thought. Nor were they purely years of study. We had ample opportunity to assimilate it all and let our spiritual life profit from it in prayer and meditation. I sincerely hope that all of this has left its mark in my life and activities. As Jesuits spend such long years studying we are usually ordained after the third year of theology. I chose a Sunday in August, 1954, for my ordination which took place in Stockholm. It was indeed a day that I had been looking forward to.

The years at Heythrop were interesting and pleasant. We did not spend all our time studying but were able to get in a lot of outdoor life, such as bicycle tours in the Cotswolds and plenty of sports. Soccer was a favourite game and I used to play goalie, not an easy position as there were several good forwards around. One of them had been an international for the West Indies, and a Spaniard had been offered a professional contract. He could shoot equally hard with either foot and managed to dribble through the defence, using only his head, a feat that I have never seen anyone else achieve.

For relaxation we indulged in music and theatre (our own productions), bridge and monthly films, not to mention literature. I ploughed my way through English 19th century novels by Jane Austen, Thackeray, Brontë, Hardy, Trollope and others. The old Heythrop manor was a fitting place to make such acquaintances. At times I thought I could hear the grinding wheels of an approaching coach and imagined an unmarried daughter hastening to peer through the curtains to see if John Knightley, Esq., had just arrived to pay his respects to her father.

Chapter 15

With Lepers and poor Andalusians in Spain

I was now ready for tertianship, or the last year of formation offered a Jesuit after the long years of study. It is a period of reflection and spiritual renewal to rekindle the fervour of the novitiate, but in a more mature form. We studied the rules of the Jesuit order and its history, read many books about the spiritual life and, once again, spent a whole month praying and meditating on the spiritual exercises of St. Ignatius.

There was a marked difference from the novitiate: we were now all ordained priests and could be given practical experience in pastoral work. I was to spend this last year in Spain, which I had never visited before. It gave me the chance to get firsthand experience of the Mediterranean way of being a Catholic — something many in northern Europe tend to be supercilious about — and also learn the language properly, which stood me in good stead later, as many Latin American exiles later settled in Sweden.

In the 1950's, there were so many Spanish Jesuits that there were three houses for the tertianship. I chose the one in Gandía, a small town south of Valencia, surrounded by orange orchards. Springtime in Gandiá was wonderful, with the perfume of the orange blossoms pervading the whole area. The beach was untouched and inviting; today it is covered with hotels and has become a favourite resort for people from Madrid.

However, we young Jesuit priests had not come for a vacation, and the venerable Father Segarra, our tertian master, did not approve of us going for a swim, nor were we supposed to read a daily newspaper. At the same time, he was open-minded enough not interfere with any one who did not keep strictly to such rules, had a comprehensive knowledge of the Jesuit order and gave us good advice on matters spiritual.

We lived in an annex of the renaissance palace that had belonged to the Borja family, known in Italy as Borgia. It was from these parts that the ill-reputed pope Alexander VI came, and his eldest son was the first duke of Gandía. Not exactly a model for young Jesuits, but we concentrated our attention on the fourth duke, Francisco de Borja, a governor of Catalonia, who after the death of his wife joined the Jesuits, became the third general of the Society of Jesus, and was even canonized as a saint. He tried to make up for some of the faults of his forebears (his maternal grandfather, an archbishop of Zaragossa, was the son of another archbishop of Zaragossa, who in his turn was the illegitimate son of king Ferdinand).

* * *

During the tertianship, we are asked to do two 'experiments', as Ignatius calls them, one at a hospital and one in a parish during Lent. These two periods are what I remember most vividly from that year in Spain.

During the hospital experiment, we normally worked as orderlies, as they say in the army, or as assistants helping with the chores. In our case it was somewhat different as we were sent to Fontilles, a leper colony founded by Spanish Jesuits. What, lepers in Spain? It is easy to forget that it was as late as 1873 that a Norwegian physician in Bergen identified the bacteria (since then leprosy has been called the Hansen disease). In the 1950's, there were some 8,000 people in Spain suffering from the disease. Thanks to the discovery of sulpha, it is now possible to arrest the development of the illness, which, unfortunately, does not mean eliminating the damages already caused. Many lepers could therefore be treated as out-patients, but there were still three leper colonies in the country.

Fontilles is located south of Gandía, in the direction of Alicante, but some miles inland in a typical Spanish mountain region, arid and not very inviting. Arriving there after darkness, we saw nothing of the buildings or of the patients that evening. I was asked to take the 8 o'clock Mass next morning. The medical staff attended in a side chapel and received Holy Communion from a chalice reserved for them.

The priest then went back to the main altar to fetch another chalice, from which Communion was distributed to the sick, who had gathered along the altar rail.

I had never met a leper before but had been imbued with the common dread of being struck by it (I never dared to tell my parents about Fontilles). From the altar, I had only had a general impression of the sick. Now I saw them close up, as they were kneeling to receive Communion. It was a heart-rending sight. I saw fingers that could not fold in prayer because they lay twisted back on the upper part of their hands; gaping holes instead of a nose, and those eyes — some of them dried out, so that the pupil looked like a shrivelled-up pea on a stalk, sticking out of an empty socket, while others spread out like the contents of a broken egg.

They opened their mouths so that I could put the sacred Host on their tongues. Never before, or afterwards, have I had such face to face confrontation with human misery and suffering. My heart opened up to them, yet at the same time it tightened, out of compassion, and out of fear of being infected. There was only one thing to do: to get on with it, to give them Holy Communion, where Our Lord Himself had become present under the sign of bread; to ask Him to comfort and help them, while at the same time telling Him that if You have sent me here, You had better help me through it. A priest (or a doctor or nurse for that matter) must not imagine that he is going to be struck by all the illnesses and misery that he meets — or that he is going to be able to alleviate or remove all of it.

During the following weeks, I was to see many patients going through a much more active state of the illness, with high fever and acute pain. Our primary duty was to get to know as many of the patients as possible and try to comfort them and cheer them up. You might think that this was a heavy task, but the atmosphere in Fontilles was extraordinary. When a visiting Brazilian inquired how many suicides we had annually, the physician in charge just looked surprised and said: "Suicides? Not a single one all through the years."

We young Jesuits were the ones to be edified and encouraged by the sick, who represented all ages and backgrounds. There was doña Carmen from a well-to-do family in the

Philippines, who had had to leave husband and three children behind. A prioress from a convent, a farmer's wife, young gypsy boys, who liked to dance a flamenco for us.

And then there was Concha. A tiny woman, not yet 40, but badly scarred by the illness. She had had a tracheotomi, that is a small incision below the larynx, to overcome breathing problems. But what a wonderful disposition she had, and such a sense of humour. She had to cover the small hole with her thumb when talking or smoking a cigarette. Concha is a nickname for Concepción, which gives you the association of the Virgin Mary and her Immacualte Conception. But Concha was anything but immaculate. The illness had left her face disfigured by scars, and she told me about her profession — she had been a prostitute in Melilla, the Spanish enclave in North Africa. She recounted being taken out to a restaurant and always ordering minced meat. The officer would suggest something else, but Concha did not budge and she told me why: "You see, Father, I had never learnt to handle both knife and fork, and I did not want to make a fool out of myself in front of them." Now, in spite of all her difficulties, she never uttered a word of complaint or even showed impatience, except when she happened to be out of cigarettes.

Teresa was a bit older, around fifty. Like many of the other patients, she had had a hard time before coming to Fontilles. Lepers have always been more or less outcasts. At Fontilles, Teresa had a room with a bed in it, food to eat, clothes, nurses and doctors to attend to her needs and she was member of a large community of several hundred persons. True, they lived in an enclosed area, which they could not leave without permission, but Teresa did not feel that as a restriction. Occasionally, she would receive visitors from home, but I am certain that she told them the same thing that she told me: "Fontilles, that is paradise on earth as far as I am concerned." And her face lit up as she said it.

I was sorry to have to return to the normal routine in Gandía when my two weeks were up. But as luck would have it there was a vacancy later on, and I could spend another fortnight in Fontilles. I would not have exchanged my time there for anything else, least of all for a holiday at a fashionable Spanish seaside resort.

There were two tabus in Fontilles. One was laid down by the patients: you could talk openly about everything, including the suffering caused by the disease, but you were not to call it by its proper name. The correct way was to refer to it as la enfermedad, the illness, not use the word leprosy. The other tabu emanated from those responsible for the colony: we were advised never to touch the patients in order to avoid the danger of infection. However, we soon found out that shaking hands with them gave them the greatest of pleasure, and we ignored the rule.

As a matter of fact, leprosy is not as contagious as we have been led to believe. During the many years that Fontilles had existed, no member of the staff had ever contracted the disease and the doctor in charge told me that he did not know how the disease spreads. He had made many experiments to find an answer, all with negative results, though it included making an intravenal injection on himself with blood taken from a patient in an active stage of leprosy. This might seem foolhardy, but should perhaps rather be termed courageous, as the doctor knew that nowadays, it is possible to arrest the progress of the illness with the help of sulpha.

According to an estimate made some decades ago there are about 15 million lepers in the world. A French physician, Raoul Follereau, who spent much of his life fighting leprosy, once had a good idea. As the president of the USA and the Soviet leader were to meet, he sent them telegrams, asking both of them to strike one fighter aircraft off the next year's budget and spend the money on sulpha instead. He more or less promised them that the suffering caused by leprosy could then be stopped and the disease practically eradicated worldwide.

Did he get his money? No, he did not even get an answer to his telegrams. Nor did the media bother to take up his cause. If they had, they could probably have forced the statesmen to accept his proposal, out of shame, if the pressure on them had been strong enough. But there was no Bob Geldorf to make a song and dance about it.

Today, there are not many lepers left, in Spain at least, but the world has a new form of leprosy to contend with — AIDS. At the time of writing, there is still no remedy for it, and it might take years before we know how to cure it. I cannot help reacting against the way people talk about AIDS, and that goes both for suggestions of how to avoid contracting the disease and the way people behave towards those who have been struck by it.

An information sheet from the Swedish Board of Health depicts a young couple listing their previous partners. The sum total is 23. The only advice proffered is: Use prophylactics. Quite apart from the moral aspect, it would seem more reasonable to suggest a certain amount of self-discipline.

But what is worse is the hysterical way people react when confronted with some one who is an AIDS carrier — he is treated like an outcast. Even the police insist on being protected against them. When a person is about to be arrested, it is enough for him to tell the officer "I've got AIDS and I'll bite you" to cause a minor panic.

The Catholic archbishop of New York, Cardinal O'Connor, was made a member of the presidential committee for AIDS. No one can accuse him of laxity in his moral teaching or of encouraging the type of sexual behaviour that is likely to spread the disease. But he became shocked over the way people behave towards the victims: "They are dying, and we treat them like killers". When Pope John Paul II met a group of AIDS victims during his visit to San Francisco in 1987, he was unable to find timely words to alleviate their problem. But he embraced them as brethren.

Francis FitzGerald has described life in Ashbury Haight, San Francisco, in articles in The New Yorker and in a book, and it is anything but pleasant reading. But I have also read about people afflicted by AIDS who gather together, knowing that their time will soon be up. The way they prepare themselves to meet their Maker is often very edifying and they certainly need all our help and our prayers. Mother Teresa of Calcutta, who has specialised in preparing people for heaven, has founded homes for AIDS patients, both in San Francisco and in New York City. Her efforts will by no means be enough, but they are a reminder to us all about the great need that exists to help the lepers of today.

* * *

During Lent, we were sent out to help out in various parishes. After a week in the Jesuit residence in Malaga hearing confessions (and getting used to the Andalusian accent) I went to Gibralgalia, some 30 miles north of Malaga, near Pizarra. Now 'near' is not the right word, because I had to get off the bus in the middle of the road, where a man met me with a mule, which was to carry him, myself and my luggage up the mountain paths to the isolated village. Don't listen to any one who speaks in a disparaging way about donkeys and mules: they are incredibly patient and strong animals, and life in these regions would be next to impossible without them.

In 1957, Gibralgalia and the surrounding districts, which I was also to visit, had a population of around 1,000. On paper they belonged to the parish of Pizarra, but the priest hardly ever showed up in the village. I am afraid he was not an exception. There were many priests in Spain, but they generally preferred to stay in the urban areas, this was even true of the Jesuits. One of them, however, Father Tiburcio Arnaiz, had realized the plight of the people in the countryside and in 1922, he encouraged Maria Isabel Gonzalez del Valle to start a rural mission. Thus the Obras de las doctrinas rurales was founded, and members of this group had even prepared the ground for my Lenten mission.

There was a small chapel in the village, but no regular Mass. No school, no electricity, no roads, just winding paths. The postman arrived on a donkey, but he had few letters to distribute, as hardly anyone in the village knew how to read and write.

A small house was placed at my disposal. When I entered it, a cluster of children trailed me, eager to have a look at the strange priest, dressed in a black suit instead of a cassock. They inspected everything that I unpacked, item for item. "What is this?" An alarm clock, a tooth brush — unknown objects. My greatest hit was a small portable radio receiver. No one had ever seen or listened to one before.

There were wooden shutters but no windows in the hut, a dirt floor and no modern conveniences. Water had to be fetched from one of the few village wells. There were no drains. For nature calls, there was a simple solution: you went to the neighbour's stable and squatted next to the mules and donkeys (hoping they would refrain from kicking you at that particular moment).

This was to be my headquarters for more than a month.

For the first and last time in my life, I kept a diary, which I reproduce in order to let the reader share some of my experiences. I have generally kept the terse form in which it was written. The "señoritas" stand for the members of the rural mission.

30:3 Mass in Arroyo in a small house at the foot of the mountain. They offer me something refreshing in the hot weather: sliced oranges with salt and rancid olive oil!

Confessions. First the women, then the men. Cristòbal, 72, has probably not been to the sacraments since his wedding. Does not really remember any prayers, but when he manages to fill in a word or two, he is quite proud: " 'cos I like religion, padre". The señoritas take it for granted that no one knows the common prayers and I notice them asking every one fresh from confession what they got for penance, and then recite it out loud with them. Consequently, I give every penitent one Our Father to say, so that no one will start wondering why one penitent got more penance than the other.

Mass indoors. Over the table used as an altar there is a reproduction of a semi-nude. Up in front, more natural, a mother gives the breast to her child. They sing something with flamenco rhythm.

2 a.m. Our things are loaded on to a donkey, and with the help of a storm lamp, we find our way back up the steep, winding path. Coffee is served on arrival, we chat. I get to sleep at 5 a.m.

Two hours later — bang, bang on the door. "What, padre is still asleep?" Some children just wanted to say hello.

8 p.m. A wedding. The señoritas help to dress the bride (and later tell me that she is wearing three petticoats). The chapel is packed. We cheer the newly-weds and continue with the bridal Mass. It is hot and sultry, many candles and lights are burning. With all her petticoats, the bride is ready to swoon.

Afterwards, there is a wedding feast in the tavern, with flamenco songs, guitars and dancing.

1.4. Mass at 9 a.m. On my way to the chapel, I pass the centre of the village where men are standing around idle, just as in the Gospel. Very few have a steady job. Every morning a foreman from a large estate or a local farmer arrives to engage day-labourers, paying them the mimimum wage of 33 pesetas (about one dollar). Come harvest time, the men can stay at home, while the women are enrolled for even less money. Have they already forgotten that there was a revolution in this country less than 20 years ago?

Visiting the sick at home. Juan, 80, embraces and kisses me. Lice crawl in the bedclothes, but fortunately they ignore me. Amelita is a bit sceptical at first, then happy after confession.

There is a new-born baby in the house. Her brother sleeps on the floor, with a sack for bedding. A small girl hides under the bed.

2.4. An old woman of 92 sits outside the house as I pass by. We chat and she is full of vigour and life, offers to dance a flamenco for me, if I so wish.

More visits to the sick. I am surprised how many have managed to get to church on their own.

"Watch out for that mule, he is vicious!" How come? "Well, he has a sore on the back. As soon as I unload, he all right again." Couldn't you let him rest a few days until the sore is healed? "No, I can't spare the money."

I make a second visit to anoint a sick man, who is now close to death. This morning the house was filthy, now it is clean and the walls have been white-washed. The neighbours help out.

3.4. Must prepare the mission in Malagueños. Not easy to preach 5, 6 sermons in Spanish. But this is the only time during the year that they see a priest.

The señoritas and their helper start piling things on to the poor donkey. Bedclothing, mass kit, food. On top of everything four benches for the temporary chapel! But the donkey does not complain, even though it has to keep its head low, so as not to hit it against the benches. It has got used to the señoritas and their crazy ways... They get away four hours late, so I wait until 7 p.m. before leaving. A message arrives: "Don't expect much of a welcome at Malagueños." Just what I needed — to have to preach to people who do not want to listen.

It is a good hour's walk to Malagueños, a cluster of homesteads, mostly belonging to members of the same family. The houses are somewhat larger and better built than those in Gibralgalia. Not quite the same poverty. The family where I stay own four mules, housed in the stables next to my room, with a connecting hatch-door. Crunch, crunch. . . splash, splash, all night long. Pling, plong from the bell of the leader of the flock. Chicken, pigs and goats add minor noises, while some watchdogs have stronger lungs. The fleas have just a short way to my bed, but this time, I had not forgotten to bring along the DDT.

4.4. At 8.30 a.m., the señoritas shoot off crackers to remind the people that there is to be a sermon at 9.30. Second set of crackers at 10 a.m. Half an hour later, a few have arrived. At 10.50, I start with an audience of about a dozen. Several are children, three of them sleep.

I make house calls. A grandmother, 82, is in good form, but refuses to go to confession. "We did not get a blessing for the house four years ago, as my sons were living in sin." Soy mujer caprichiosa — I do things the way I feel like.

Sermon for women at 5 p.m., which means 7.15 p.m. They come when they have finished working, when it seems right. No one has a watch, so time is approximate.

Evening sermon for everybody, indoors. There is a good crowd. I remind them that the following evening, there will be a Mass. Of course, I know that Friday is the day you meet your novia/novio (the day for dating), and obviously it is easier to love the girl you see than God, whom you don't see. . . But it is Lent, make a sacrifice and come to Mass. They listen and seem to accept my message.

After the sermon, they ask me to switch on the radio, but are disappointed as the music broadcast is by Rachmaninov: "What a pity, we prefer flamenco!"

5.4. Mass is to be celebrated in a newly built house. It rains today — hurray! Never mind that the roof leaks a bit.

More house calls. The paths are dirty in the rain, so I tuck my trousers into my socks, borrow a pair of alpargatas (local straw sandals) and carry an umbrella. An old woman sits in the doorway, sewing, and laughs at my appearance. We have quite an enjoyable chat together. Finally, I suggest that as a gesture of thanksgiving for the rain, she could make her East duties. She pretends not to understand until her son comes to my assistance but then declares: "I don't want to!"

I look surprised. We have been getting on so well together. She tries a dodge — it has not rained enough to be grateful. "What, do you want to drown in water first?" I ask. This sets her laughing, she chases the sons out of the house and gets on with her confession. Afterwards she seems pleased.

Before Mass, I visit a neighbour, but the wife says she is in mourning (her daughter died several months ago) so she cannot leave the house, not even to cross the road. Just as in Lorca's play The House of Bernarda Alba. Most of the young people attend the evening Mass, both novios and novias. I use the new house as a setting for my sermon: we are to be the temple of God. The stairs lead to the upper level — with God's help, we are one day to get to heaven. They listen and seem to get my point. Concrete examples are important, especially with my poor Spanish. Almost everyone receives Holy Communion.

I get to bed at 1.30 a.m. but feel a cold coming on, so I take some aspirins against the fever. Two hours later, I wake up. I am riddled with fleas, my pyjamas are soaking, there is a puddle of sweat and DDT in the bed. From next door, I hear grown-ups talking and children crying. Dawn is not far away when I managed to get back to sleep, and I wake up exausted.

More sick Communions, three yesterday, six today. The rain continues, so they let me ride, but returning, I almost fall asleep on the mule. After lunch, we pack and return to Gibralgalia. I decline the offered animal. It is better to walk and keep warm.

8.4. The sick man I anointed has died, so I visit the family. The house is dirty again, and the inhabitants in rags which hardly cover them. The only proper clothes they have are now being dyed black.

9.4. On the way back from Monjos, we meet people who have come down from Gibralgalia in order to do their washing in the stream. Half an hour's walk. Lydia and I help them carry some of the laundry back to the village. In exchange, our baskets, filled with lettuce, peas and artichokes (a gift, which we helped to gather in the field) are loaded onto their donkey.

I have my usual fight with the señoritas about carrying things. To them, a priest must not be seen carrying anything, whereas I feel that the man, not the women, should do the carrying. We have arrived at a compromise: I am allowed to carry the rucksack between the villages, but as soon as we meet any one, I have to hand it over to them.

12.4. I devote more time to the men in the village, chatting, smoking with them. Several have been to Vitoria or Madrid to work. In Malaga and large parts of the South, there is little industry.

13.4. Mass at Los Ranchos, and I ride with Pedro el Cojo (the lame). Would prefer to be alone on the horse, but they are a bit doubtful if I can manage on my own. The heavy load makes it even more difficult for the animal as the "road" is a steep and stony path. Some 20 − 30 persons come to Mass. Afterwards, Pedro mounts his horse, but a stray dog starts chasing him, and he falls off, crutches and all. The saddle girth has broken and we have an uneasy ride back home.

14.4. Mass at Alajara. They send a horse and this time, I dispose of it alone. There are 97 persons in the small house and I hear confessions until 1 a.m. before the Mass can start.

15.4. A shy shepherd boy, about 13, stands apart from the crowd. He is afraid to go to confession. So I pick him up and carry him under my arm away from the villagers, who start laughing. He is not scared, quite the contrary, and now willing to go to confession. Mass is outdoors, people stand around, the children sit on the ground.

16.4. Mission at Merinos. Mass is to be celebrated in a large house, but the atmosphere is unpleasant. The owners are at loggerheads with their neighbours, having taken a different stand during the civil war. It is too late to move to a neutral house. I visit the people next door and plead, reminding them that this is the only Mass this year in this location. But neither side is willing to give an inch. They are full of ugly hate, which makes me feel sick, even physically.

10 p.m. I start with a sermon on love of your neighbour. Then confessions. The local women insist on having a rib-backed chair as a makeshift confessional. More people

arrive. We are around 50 when Mass starts at 0.45 a.m.

I am glad when it is over. We load the donkey, and I walk home, arriving in Gibralgalia at 3.15, get to bed at 4 a.m. Before falling to sleep, I wonder if I have been too hard on the people at Merino. But I do feel that hate is worse than most other sins.

Maundy Thursday. I discuss the decoration of the chapel with the señoritas. They want to build a tomb for Jesus in front of the altar, before the Mass starts. I insist on space for the liturgy, including the washing of the feet, suggesting that the tomb be placed on the side. Lydia is close to tears, frustrated by the padre intransigente, but I don't give in to her.

Confession for children. Quite a few come, also grown-ups, and I spent two hours hearing confessions.

Today being one of the few holidays when all the men stay in the in the village, I go to visit them at the taverna. Mostly for a lark, I tell them that they can help me to find out if every one has prepared for Easter by going to confession. They take it up and start pointing: here is one who hasn't been yet, there is another. I approach these two and, with a smile, tell them: "OK, leave the glass on the table for a while and come with me." Surprisingly enough, they do, and are not annoyed. In the evening, they both appear at Mass and receive Communion.

Maundy Thursday liturgy. Washing of the feet. The señoritas want to select some small boys, but I prefer adult men to represent the apostles. I win again... There is only room for eight of them. They have washed their feet today, an unusual hygenic procedure for people in these primitive surroundings. So the señoritas bring me hot water, soap and proper towels. I wash with such success that they have to change the water three times for the eight men, making it a most meaningful ceremony.

Good Friday. At 3 p.m, I finish confessions and we can start the liturgy. Yesterday there were 230 communicants, today there are 170; many children feel they have done their share, but almost all the men come again.

7.30 p.m. Procession, via dolorosa, stations of the cross. For more than an hour, they carry a heavy crucifix (with bobbinet for a shroud) and a statue of Virgen de la Soledad (the desolate Mother) up and down our miserable paths, real hard work. We stop every now and then for a prayer, and someone sings a genuine saeta, not the commercial variety. The Arab melody is full of lament.

23.4 The last day. Mass at 7.15, donkey ride to Arroyo de Membrillo, sick communion to an old couple, he 80, she 70. They got married 50 years ago, and he has not been to the sacraments since. "Do I pray at all? Well, not much. But my wife, she prays a lot."

That apparently, is enough for the whole family, and I suppose it is good enough for the Lord, too.

* * *

The year in Spain is drawing to a close and I can finally return home to start working as a priest in Sweden.

What did I see of Franco's Spain? Not that much, but I did get the impression that there was great need for social reforms. Still, as long as the country was isolated and ostracised by the rest of Europe, it was not easy to change things. 20 more years were to pass until the end of the Franco era. I have not returned to Gibralgalia, but I suppose that time has finally caught up with it.

One final reflection: The people of Gibralgalia were practically all illiterates when I was there. As the media, such as newpapers and radio, were not available to them, they were not handed ready made comments and conclusions, but had to think things out for themselves. I met many wise philosophers, both men and women, who had reflected a lot and were willing to share their thoughts with others. Don't mark me down as an advocate for illiteracy. But it does make you think.

I got in a certain amount of tourism: the Alhambra palace in Granada, the exquisite mosque/cathedral in Cordova, the crater city of Guadix, where the church, as well as the count's palace, are underground grottos, having been carved out of the soft volcanic stone. There was Madrid, of course, but I skipped the Prado museum, having seen the cream of the collection several times when it was exhibited in Geneva in 1939 prior to being sent back to Spain after the civil war.

El Escorial I found as sombre as the way Philip II is depicted in a biography by the German writer Reinhold Schneider. But Avila was a medieval gem, and I would not have been surprised if I had run into Saint Teresa in the middle of the street. In Loyola, it rained, and I almost felt grateful to get away from the eternal sunshine.

I was definitely on my way home.

Chapter 16

Working as a Catholic Priest in Sweden

With the year in Spain my training as a Jesuit had ended. Eleven years had passed since I had entered the novitiate but I never had time to get bored as I, spent them in different places studying a variety of subjects. The only burden was to keep on studying when most of my contemporaries were already active in their chosen professions. During the final years, however, I had been an ordained priest and had been able to gain experience working in large parishes in Great Britain, Western Germany and Spain before getting back home where everything Catholic was small-sized.

The first three years in Sweden (1957 – 60) I spent at the parish of St. Eugenia in Stockholm. The church was located in a side street near NK, the large department store, but has since disappeared in the upheavals that preceded the renovation of the city. It has been replaced by a modern shopping centre. Although going back no further than to the year of 1837, St. Eugenia's church was historically interesting as the first Catholic church to be erected in Sweden after the Reformation. There even used to be an official notice at the entrance forbidding Swedish Catholics to attend services — the edict of tolerance from 1781 applied to foreigners only. It owed its existence to the benevolence of queen Josephine, née Beauharnais, who was married to king Oscar II of the new Bernadotte dynasty. Her chaplain, J.L. Studach, was consecrated bishop and as Vicar Apostolic was responsible for the few Catholics in Sweden and Norway.

In this church I had been ordained a priest on 22 August 1954, also an historical event as I was the first Swedish-born Jesuit ever to be ordained and allowed to function as a priest in Sweden. The press took it up and I remember seeing photographers leaning out of the pulpit to get good pictures. In their reports they talked about the first Swedish Jesuit since the Reformation, forgetting that the Society of Jesus was not established until 1540.

* * *

In the 1950's the Catholic Church in Sweden was small. There were only 7 — 8 000 Catholics in the country at the end of the Second World War, divided into nine parishes, three of them in Stockholm. From 1873 onwards Swedish citizens could obtain permission to pass from the Lutheran state church to another Christian church. You could not just leave it and be an atheist officially, and if you wanted to transfer to say the Jewish Community, your case had to be approved by the King in council. Those who were not members of the Lutheran church were excluded from certain professions such as teachers of elementary schools and I know of two Catholic Swedish women who were refused entry into nursing training colleges. One of them appealed to the prince Carl, a brother of the king and president of the Red Cross, but even that was of no avail.

Anyone wishing to leave the Lutheran Church had to appear in person to the pastor in charge of his parish and be admonished about falling away from the true religion to become a heretic. If you came back after three months and persisted in your intentions, your request could be approved. Such was the situation until 1952 when a new law of religious tolerance was enacted. It is a sign rather of secularization than of tolerance, however, as was evident from the acrid debates in the parliament, especially when it came to the question allowing convents and monasteries to be established again.

There was still much anti-Catholic prejudice in the air. Patriots looked back on the 17th century when Sweden had been a major power in Europe. King Gustavus Adolphus who in 1632 died fighting the German emperor was considered a martyr for the Lutheran faith. To embrace the Catholic faith had been considered almost the same as becoming a renegade. Some friends of my mother fed her with 'true' stories, which she often believed. One day she told me about a large boarding school in Rome established exclusively for the illegitimate children of priests, monks and nuns. I asked her to find out from her friends its exact location and suggested that she get a prospectus for it. "Who knows, I might be in need of it one day", I said but added: "I won't deny that priests and nuns may have children. But can you imagine anyone being so stupid as to bunch them all together in one place and hang out a sign telling everyone about it?" From that day on she queried the stories served up to her and even starting defending my faith, without knowing much about it.

In the early 1950's, a well-known figure in the Swedish world of culture came to call on Fr. Gerlach in Uppsala with tears in his eyes, having been told that his son intended to become a Catholic. "Have you explained to him that it means renouncing all of his Swedish cultural heritage?" asked the professor. Yet at this time a number of well-known Swedes in the world of culture had found their way to the Catholic Church. Some of them were influenced by French Catholic culture which they wrote about in books and newspaper articles. This has resulted in a widespread opinion that Catholicism is mainly for intellectuals. It would be more correct to state that a Swede needed courage and determination to become a Catholic.

* * *

After World War II, migration became common in Europe and as a result of it, a number of Catholics started arriving in Sweden. They came from camps in Austria, from Italy, Spain and Yugoslavia. At first they were not allowed to reside in the four major cities and were settled in outlying districts where there were no other Catholics. Some years later, exiles started arriving after the revolts in Hungary (1956), Czechoslovakia (1968) and then from Latin America, especially Chile, to be followed by a great number of Poles and finally people from the Middle East. The growing number of Catholics made heavy demands on the one and only bishop in Sweden, who had to find priests to look after them and erect new parishes around the country. This entailed finding means to finance the expansion and the bishop would spend many months every year travelling in the USA and West Germany to make appeals for the needs of his diocese. In the middle of the 1970's, the government finally start giving minor subsidies to support religious activities outside the state church.

When I arrived in Stockholm in 1957 my main work was in the parish. We tried to visit the parishioners at home, which was much easier in those days when there was hardly any television at all. It was taken for granted that the faithful had more patience then and I was told that the sermon at high Mass on Sundays should last at least half an hour. (Today they say you can preach over anything except ten minutes.) There was some consternation when one day I quoted the Swedish equivalent of The Punch in my sermon. A member of the congregation came up to me saying that she wanted to go to confession as she had laughed in church. I replied that if I tell a funny story in the pulpit and you do not laugh, that's when you go to confession.

Having become acquainted with religion in the Anglo-Saxon world, it was obvious to me that humour is a vital part of it, whereas the worst heresy of Swedes is that religion must be solemn to the point of being boring. I do not know if Luther's ideas about man's debility after the Fall or the strict views of some non-conformists are to be blamed for this, but most Swedes seem to think that mirth and religion do not mix. Playing cards was considered sinful, not to mention dancing (which I had enjoyed too much. Upon becoming a Jesuit, I gave it up, a real sacrifice. My friends in the 90th Field Security Section, who knew of my intentions, used to call me Larry the jitterbugging monk).

Let me give you a couple of examples: Together with a Jesuit friend I visited a great-aunt aged 94. She did not speak English and my friend Ron knew no Swedish so I talked alternatively to one or the other of them. At one point Ron and I (both wearing Roman collars) started laughing out loud. The great-aunt look scandalized and asked: "Are you being wicked now?" On another occasion I visited my brother, who normally does not show much interest in religion. In the course of the conversation I twisted a biblical phrase to make a joke. My brother look horrified and told me: "Lars, it is not proper to say things like that."

My cousins had a grandmother who more or less terrorized them with her piety. On a rainy Sunday afternoon, one of the cousins was playing solitaire when the door opened. Fortunately it was her aunt (my mother) and not grannie. With tremor in her voice, my cousin asked: "Do you think that

God will punish me if I play this patience once more?"

As head of the Scandinavian section of the Vatican Radio, I make programmes for "average" Swedish listeners and we regularly receive letters expressing surprise that we do not refrain from cracking jokes in our transmissions (or playing jazz music). They have been brought up to consider such behaviour unseeming in a person who professes to be "religious".

I wish they could have seen the show that the young people of Sydney put on for the Pope in 1986. A famous pop singer was the leading star and master of ceremonies. There was sparkling display of song and music, of dance and colours. The Pope's message to them was both serious and encouraging. But he also watched their dancing and listened to their music; joined in their singing and ended up being dragged along in a serpentine dance and hugging the main performers. Maybe the young people remembered this part better than his words. Preaching as well as singing and dancing with the youth seemed to come quite natural to him and why shouldn't it? Man is one and indivisible and we must give evidence of this unity. Religion is not a diffuse "need" that can be relegated to Sundays and sacristies. Our consciousness of the Lord and his message of joy should bubble over and become evident in our whole lifestyle.

The religion that is of no use on weekdays is of even less use on a Sunday.

Now I cannot deny that some Catholics recommend austerity too. When in Spain I got into a discussion with the old father in charge of the tertianship about a certain French Jesuit, père Ginhac, who had been famous for asceticism. He fell for the temptation to keep exact account of all his virtuous exercises. He spent such long hours praying at night that he found it difficult to keep awake when talking to his students. The old Spanish father accepted some of my criticism but countered with the thought that "he was so edifying. Fancy, once going on a train journey, he found the carriages full of noisy people. Seeing him entering their compartment, a woman admonished the others saying: 'Hush, a saint is coming our way.' Wasn't that edifying?" asked the old father.

I am afraid I did not agree and I told him that in a similar situation, I would prefer someone saying: "Oh, look it's you, come on in and join us!" Several years later I was reminded of my remark when travelling by train from Stockholm to Uppsala. One of our students was in an adjoining compartment and he came looking for me saying: "I heard that laughter and decided it had to be you." Old Fr. Segarra was a sensible man and I trust that he would have found this episode edifying also.

* * *

After a while I found myself spending a fair amount of time in the Royal library of Stockholm reviewing the period when Sweden was swept up by the Reformation. Until then, only Protestants had written about it and they seemed happy about the fact that the Swedes had seen the true light in 1537 at the parliament of Västerås. As a Catholic I found it difficult to be as enthusiastic as they were and also asked myself: "Do things happen that suddenly?" What was the state of religion in Sweden prior to the Reformation? Did the local church really need shaking up that badly?

My superior decided that I was to be given the opportunity to delve more deeply into the questions and in October 1960, I was transferred to Uppsala. Fr. Gerlach, who in 1945 had helped me to decide for the Jesuits, was still there and we became good friends. He had spent many years on a lonely post holding the fort for the Catholics in a city dominated by the University and living near the residence of the Lutheran archbishop.

I had already committed the main line of argument to writing and submitted it to an historical seminar but afterwards moved on to Sten Lindroth, professor of the history of science and ideas and a member of the Swedish Academy. He was a most stimulating lecturer and I have never run into anyone else who appeared to be so full of enthusiasm whatever the subject of the lecture was. He helped me to find a focal figure for my investigations, a cleric by the name of Sveno Jacobi, who had studied in Louvain and was undoubtedly a good representative for new thoughts propounded there by Erasmus and his friends. Sveno made a career right up to the top in the king's chancelry and was rewarded with a bishopric in Skara.

The king, Gustav Vasa, after having liberated Sweden

from Danish hegemony, had favoured Lutheran ideas, especially those which looked upon the King as head of both the
state and the church. He thus felt justified to confiscate lands
belonging to the church and to appoint bishops and clerics
without reference to Rome. However, when he appointed
a German Lutheran as minister of church affairs and had
him ransack the local parish churches for most of their
belongings, Sveno protested and was demoted to dean. There
was a sizeable collection of letters to and from Sveno, mostly
inedited, as well as other interesting material to work on. I
spent a lot of time in the university library studying and
trying to decipher letters in Latin and old Swedish. It was
not easy and I usually had severals queries, which even the
experts could not cope with.

When I collected all my notes to write up a thesis on
Sveno and his times, I noticed that there were many gaps
in the material available. Even his last letter, in which he
admonished a disciple for accepting an important church
appointment by the King, had vanished from the collection.
In the end I had to abandon my project, seeing that too many
important links were missing. I could console myself that
many other students did not manage to finish their thesis.
Yet the years of study at the university had by no means been
wasted. Catholic priests are rare birds in Sweden and people
expect them to be able to answer questions about many
subjects, especially if you are a Jesuit, who is supposed to be
a man of learning. So we have to be what I call professional
dilettants, and I hope that Sten Lindroth will not turn in the
grave if I state that he helped me a bit along that road.

Finally a little true story about my professor. We were
having a bite to eat after a seminar and Lindroth started
talking about his doctoral thesis on Paracelsus. Lindroth did
not care for the mysticism of Paracelsus and criticized his
nebulous views on qualities. But fortunately, he concluded,
Galilei arrived on the scene and swept all that away, talking
about mathematics and quantity instead. I could not resist
the temptation and commented: "Well, I hope that if I
manage to present a thesis to you one day, you will judge
it only by its quantity, not by its quality." As it turned out,
he did not even have to judge it by that criterion either.

* * *

Beside the studies, other tasks were beginning to take up my time. I was appointed chaplain to the Catholic students in Uppsala. There were not that many of them but it was a lively group. We lived in a period of active ecumenism and much time was spent discussing the forms in which cooperation between the various confessions could be organized. The Catholic students, being mainly converts, felt the need to get together and we met regularly for prayer, study groups and for small parties. The chaplain got to bed late and had to take the early Mass in the morning, so the students wrote a ditty:

Waking only at the Mass
longing for the bed, alas.

As a sideline, I worked for the Emmaus community in Old Uppsala, the ragpickers founded by Abbé Pierre. The men out there were almost all social dropouts with problems of alcohol so none of them had a driver's licence. I drove a small lorry around town and we picked up waste paper, bottles and old furniture, which had to be carried down steep flights of stairs. We sorted and sold whatever we got and the proceeds were sent to the Third World. More than one of the community commented that 'this is the first time in my life that I have been of any use to somebody else'.

The next extra was working for the diocesan magazine. They started out innocently by asking me to lend my name as legally responsible for it but I soon began to collaborate and became more and more involved. I travelled around Sweden visiting all the parishes, attending special events, publishing interviews and finally ended up as editor, make-up man and photographer. At the same time I was responsible for the Jesuit community and the small parish in Uppsala, looked after the Swedish programmes on the Vatican radio and gave a few courses in Uppsala and Stockholm. It was obviously too much and eventually I had to have a break after which I resumed only the work for the diocesan paper and for the Vatican Radio, more than enough to keep me out of mischief.

What I missed most was giving up the job as chaplain for the students; I had indeed enjoyed their company.

* * *

One incident from my days in Uppsala has left me with an

indelible impression: the visit of cardinal Tisserant. He was invited to Sweden in connection with a jubilee of Queen Christina's (the daughter of King Gustavus Adolfus. She abdicated the throne in 1654 to become a Catholic). It was a summer's day and I was the only priest at home and at the time, we had no sisters assisting us. The cardinal was to visit the old Cathedral (now Lutheran) before lunching at the archbishop's residence. Before leaving Uppsala, he had promised to meet the Catholic community at the Jesuit residence.

People often get nervous when they are behind schedule but that is an easy problem: you can just skip something and there you are, back on time. I found myself faced with the opposite situation. The cardinal was known to be rather short-tempered and he did not get along too well with the Lutheran archbishop for reasons on which I need not elaborate. After lunch, he finished his coffee quickly and rose saying: "I am leaving." Consternation all around. A room had been reserved for him at the archbishop's place to have a siesta and I suggested his retiring there. But the cardinal brushed it off declaring that he never took a siesta.

There is a photo of me standing in front of the Cathedral looking at my watch with a horrified expression on my face. I was two hours and a quarter ahead of schedule. What do you do to keep an irate cardinal occupied during that time? If he had insisted on going straight back to Stockholm, my Catholics would have been more than disappointed. We started by covering the short distance to the Jesuit house on foot but I soon realized that I would not be able to keep him amused there during two hours and I suggested a sightseeing trip by car, which he accepted. The cardinal and two monsignori from Rome got into our small Volkswagen beetle and I made an extensive tour of Uppsala and surroundings, returning to our residence a short time before the local Catholics were due to arrive.

Not everyone was pleased with the arrangements. I had been forced to leave all the other guests unattended at our house, including the papal delegate to Scandinavia and the Catholic bishop of Stockholm. They were not amused, but I had had to choose the lesser evil.

* * *

For several years, I was responsible for the Catholic community in Uppsala. Even though it was difficult to fulfill my
pastoral obligations fully, due to the many other demands on
my time, I looked back at parish work as most rewarding.
The cure of souls is not a subject you can write about
without breaking confidences. Still, whenever I am asked
if it is exciting to hear confessions I always answer "no".
Fortunately people do not use their phantasy to think up
new ways of sinning. Sitting in a confessional for hours on
end (as I did in Glasgow in the 1950's), I found it taxing to
be fully attentive all the time. After all, a priest attempts to
give proper advice to the penitents and it is frustrating if you
find the right words after he/she has left the confessional. It
makes you feel that you have failed both the Lord and the
penitent.

What I have found most striking is the sincerity with which
most people regret even minor faults. It makes the priest feel
ashamed that many of his parishioners are more conscien-
tious in the performance of everday duties than he is.

Chapter 17

The Turbulent Sixties

The 1960's was an eventful decennium. The Second Vatican Council (1962-65) was a time of self-examination and renewal of the Catholic Church. Simultaneously the whole world seemed to go through a rapid phase of development and this is where my attempt of analysis has to start. What was really going on?

Having been transferred to Uppsala in 1960, I saw the sixties and the ideological development mainly from the point of view of a university chaplain. It was a time of upheaval in more than one way, much of which was summarized for me one evening in the late 60's. The Christian students' associations of Uppsala had arranged a panel debate about the generation gap. I was invited to represent the oldtimers, being well over 30. A very young minister of the Lutheran church expounded the gospel according to I-don't-know whom, encouraging all to break out of the system and abolish most of the social structure. Of course he realized that the old generation would not understand what he was talking about. He and his contemporaries were the first one in Sweden to grow up with a conciousness of the whole world whereas previous generations were full of illusions, having been brought up in idyllic surroundings.

That set me off. I explained a bit about the idyll as I remembered it. In my school days the social background of the various students was most noticeable: you saw it in their shabby clothes and the school catalogue listed the profession of the father, the telephone number (if they had one) and ended with a column registering those who did not pay full fees (then about £3). I remembered the Wall Street crash in 1929, the Kreuger crash in Sweden a few years later and the unemployment situation of the 1930's. The Soviet Union grew stronger, Hitler assumed power in 1933, Mussolini invaded Abyssinia in 1935, the Spanish civil war lasted from 1936 to 1939, the year that World War II began, something that had been looming over us for years. The Russians invaded Finland that same winter and soon afterwards the Germans occupied both Norway and Denmark. Sweden just escaped a similar fate.

Since the early 1930's, the Social Democratic Party had tried to lift our population out of poverty and joblessness and give them a modicum of security and welfare, a programme that the other parties also supported. I could not see that abolishing the welfare state should have a high priority.

So much for our idyllic life. And how did we react to it? Hundreds of Swedes volunteered to fight in Spain and thousands went to help the Finns. You dub all your opponents 'Fascists'. What I did was to put on a British uniform to fight them.

And what is your reaction? I have not heard anyone even discussing the possibility of going to Vietnam as a soldier or helping out there in any other way. You stay here in the safety of the welfare state, demonstrating and protesting instead of really doing something. You must excuse me if I find it difficult to acknowledge the maturity of your commitment.

And what did they answer me? "So you were in the British Army? How cute!" (It took me a long time before I realized that a person could be grown-up and adult without having had any personal experience of World War II, a focal point in my life.)

I was not an old reactionary and my sympathies were by no means with the US in Vietnam, on the contrary. But I preferred to build opinions on facts and reacted against the emotional seas that kept sweeping over us. The most crushing reports on Vietnam I read in The New Yorker. In a series of articles on the My Lai massacre, they kept piling fact upon fact without comments, but you could feel their suppressed frustration and anger.

This detached form of reporting did not find favour with the press in Sweden. It was more important to feel indignant than to be presented with facts. Collection boxes were labelled FNL, but the students proferring them could not explain the initials, Front National de Libération being French, not English. A Chinese student in Uppsala (who was no supporter of the US cause) felt bothered by the insistence of the students soliciting contributions so she tried an experiment. Deciding that in our part of the world, people were unable to distinguish one yellow-faced person from another, she told one of them: "As I come from South Vietnam I am not interested in supporting your cause." And she commented: "I almost felt sorry for him. He become so embarrassed that he just slunk away in shame."

There were two characteristics about the late 60's that I found difficult to swallow. Everything was dead serious and you were not allowed to joke about anything. (The most rigid example I know of was the small maoistic community in Uppsala, whose members had to submit to near-torture when being drilled.) And then there was the plethora of neomarxist groups, one more dogmatic than the other. Why were Marx and Lenin suddenly so interesting? Was it a reaction against the cold war and phenomena like the McCarthyism in the USA?

Bernadette Devlin, then a member of parliament, was invited to speak to the students of Uppsala. Afterwards there were questions. One of the students commented on the situation in her country and realised that the Irish had to fight for their rights. But 'the most important thing is to form small cells and indoctrinate the members. Have you done that?' he asked.

Bernadette looked at him with a smile and said: "Well, I am afraid that the level of education in Northern Ireland is not very high. So we cannot afford the luxury of intellectual Marxism. We have to start with the basic facts." I loved her for that reply.

The Trotskyites set up their headquarters opposite our chapel and I used to chat with their boss occasionally. They had a major meeting every other Sunday when we had High Mass so one day I suggested that we might get together and take turns instead of having performances simultaneously. He looked quite shocked so I asked if his followers were so wavering about their convictions that they would not survive attending Mass every other week. At which he left me abruptly — it was not fitting to joke about such holy things.

The university Society for Foreign Affairs invited the president of Senegal, Léopold Senghor, the only African head of state at the time willing to answer questions from the audience. An African militant group took possession of the podium and the amplifying system and gave those present their views on Africa and would not let Senghor get near the microphone. Finally the organizers had to ask the police to intervene, but by that time Senghor had given up and left. The protesters were later taken to court and our Trotskyists exhorted everybody to protest against this blatant suppression of the freedom of speech. I asked my friend to clarify their position as, according to my reading, the Africans had had their say, illegally, whereas they had impeded Senghor's right to free speech. I got the dogmatically perfect answer: 'The opinions of the Africans were correct and that gave them the freedom of speech; Senghor was in the wrong and had therefore no right to utter his views.' Torequemada would have felt quite at home with that argument.

There were more subtle ways of stopping opponents. The Swedish Radio and Television Corporation had a correpondent in Rome with good connections in Eastern Europe. He went to Yugoslavia to interview Milan Djilas, an ex-friend of Tito's who had become inconvenient because of his criticism of the government. A good interview, the Swedish reporter thought, in which Djilas expressed his difficulties to understand the enthusiasm of western youth for neomarxism. "We have had our experiences here and they have not been entirely positive" he said. The tape was sent to Stockholm but happened to disappear, so the reporter went to Yugoslavia and did it all over again. But surprise, surprise, the second tape was never used, having also been lost.

Someone said that the ideology of the 60's could be compared to an intoxication, or was a substitute for religion, which could then develop into drug addiction or fancy for strange sects, preferably tainted with Eastern mysticism. It was only relatively recently that I became aware of the way the Beatles glorified LSD-trips with their grammophone record Sergeant Pepper's Band, a favourite of mine from the musical point of view.

*   *   *

Che Guevara was hailed as a saviour and the posters of him were obviously inspired by artistic representations of Jesus. Woe to anyone who dare to utter a word of criticism of Che. I fell for a while under the spell myself and when the US magazine The Rampart came out with a translation of his diary, I immediately bought it and read it from cover to cover. But what a let-down. I was all for a thorough social reconstruction of Latin America but Che's planning was all wrong. He had chosen a point in Bolivia from which the revolution was to spread and he was convinced that the local population would support him. But he failed to find out that there had been an agrarian reform recently in the area and the farmers were by no means interested in an upheaval. The whole expedition was so badly organised that they did not even have proper maps. Their small team got lost in an arid area and the engines of their jeeps started boiling. There was no water and they ended up by having to urinate into the radiator. No wonder they failed. In Colombia the university chaplain Camilo Torres became a guerilla soldier and was soon also hailed as a martyr. He was shot from behind in an ambush but as a guerilla soldier he must have used the same method himself, in spite of being a priest.

How was it possible that ideas and ideals like these took the world by storm? I cannot explain 'why' but I have a suggestion about the reasons for the 'how'. It could be one of the effects of the rapid evolution of electronics. When I left New York City in July 1943, I did not know a single person in town who owned a television set. Ten years later they became common also in Sweden. In 1957 I had been an innovator in the mountains of Andalusia with my portable radio set, but it still had valves and the batteries did not last long. Shortly afterwards the transistor conquered the world and everybody started having a radio of their own (and soon also hi-fi equipment for listening pleasure).

This led to mass movements. Disc jockeys started dishing out their music and emotional waves met the pop star idols on their world trips with teenagers milling and shouting around them, only too glad to have someone play on their heart strings. Big money saw its chance and entered the trade which soon became an industry. Soon the mass media took it up, realising that it was easier to make money playing up the sensational than giving solid and objective background information. People become used to reacting with their heart and not their head. Even catastrophes became ephemeral, to be used only as long as they sold more copies.

It is possible to use the system for good purposes — look at Bob Geldof and his campaign against the famine in Ethiopia, bringing in some fifty million pounds. But we can also be dragged into questionable company. Do you remember the Biafra war? Swedes were very proud of our daring pilot Carl Gustaf von Rosen who flew in arms and equipment to them. I got to know a medical doctor from Biafra whose Swedish wife spent the war years in Uppsala with her children. When I met him much later I asked him about the war. He told me that at the time, he risked his life on the front, being convinced that it was an attempt at genocide. Now he was equally certain that the whole thing was the result of machinations of large oil companies interested in the secession of the southern districts of Nigeria which contain the oil reserves.

* * *

Such was the mode of the world in the 1960's which was also the decade of the Second Vatican Council (1962-65). Pope John XXIII was hailed as a hero who had dared to open the windows and let in a new spring, which was a good thing and undoubtedly necessary. The key word was aggiornamento — updating the Church, which was to continue to be true to itself and its Master, but get rid of surplus ballast. In a reform of the liturgy, Latin was replaced by the vernacular. Some people thought it a pity, feeling that the solemn character of the Mass had now disappeared. They overlooked the fact that the vernacular had been on its way in centuries earlier but had been stopped by the controversies of the Reformation period.

When the Papal state was absorbed in the Risorgimento of the new and anticlerical Italy, the popes stayed inside the walls of the Vatican. It was understandable that they tended to look on the world surrounding them as an enemy and even felt virtuous about it. There was definitely need in our days of an authoritative document such as The Church in the Modern World and papal encyclicals like Mater et Magistra and On the Progress of the Nations. The council had a slow start but soon the bishops caught on and grew with the task. I am convinced that coming generations will consider the council as a good but not very daring step ahead.

The time was ripe for the Council, but unfortunately its seeds were spread in a soil where plants tended to grow wild. Catholics that previously had been proud of being different now launched into orgies of ecumenism. Solemn rites were replaced by non-sacred forms and a great number of priests, monks and nuns abandoned their traditional form of religious life, full of confidence that they would now be the real leaven of the earth and at the same time achieve realization of their true personal self.

In a book called The Runaway Church, Peter Hebblethwaite (himself a former Jesuit), described many of the resulting follies. I do not consider myself a conservative but I must admit to having run into things that made me shake my head. In 1968, I was invited to a home mass in Minneapolis, Minn., by a group of young people with a college background. They were no revolutionaries but keen on opening windows in their own religious world. I reacted somewhat over the book they were discussing, The Harrod Experiment, a novel about a college where practically all problems seemed to be solved by free sex. I do not think those present had ambitions in that direction; it was rather a reaction against the rigid way they had been taught the sixth commandment. But I definitely drew a line at participating in the Creed recited at the Mass. They had their own version and it started: "I believe in the new, in a hundred indecisions." I suppose they felt a need of freedom, having experienced a form of religion where everything was set and decided for them.

The division between progressives and conservatives has become quite pronounced also in the Church but the dividing lines are not always according to the book. There are people who are conservative in their theology but progressive in their politics and vice versa. On the whole I consider the divisions to be growing pains that seem normal after a general council. The worst part of it is the lack of charity that seems to go with lack of tolerance; that is hardly a sign of being a good Christian. When I was in charge of the diocesan paper, I was often accused of being too progressive but I took it with a smile. After all, people have dubbed Paul VI and John Paul II heretics, so I felt that I was in good company.

* * *

The sphere where I notice the effects of the Council most is ecumenism. In the Anglo-Saxon world where I had first got to know the Catholic Church, you were not only forbidden to attend a non-Catholic service. You did not even say the Our Father together because "they might mean something else by it". Swedes travelling abroad might visit Catholic churches, but they did not put their foot into one in their own country.

The great breakthrough in the Catholic Church had taken place in 1960 when the Papal Secretariate for Christian Unity was inaugurated (secretariates having been been abolished in 1989, it is now called a council). Cardinal Augustin Bea, a Jesuit who had been rector of the Biblical Institute in Rome and confessor of Pope Pius XII, was its first president, ably assisted by archbishop Willebrands, later created a cardinal and Bea's successor. Invitations were sent out to practically all Christian churches to send observers to the Second Vatican Council and Willebrands undertook many a journey to convince people to accept it. When the Moscow patriarchate said 'yes', other Orthodox churches followed. The Swedish Lutheran Church sent Sven Silén of Västerås (the only Swedish bishop who could follow the Latin discussions).

Today national and local ecumenical councils are functioning in Scandinavia and dialogue groups engage in serious theological discussion to try to understand each other and seek the way to unity. It takes time before this seeps through; what experts have agreed upon might not necessarily be accepted at the grassroot level (and vice versa). In Sweden, we have the additional difficulty of having a national Lutheran church which so far has not wanted to be disestablished. Thus final decisions regarding the creed and possible union with other churches has to be relegated to the political authority. Still, it is encouraging to find that the ecumenical climate has improved and it it important that it continue to do so. Unless

the Christian churches and communities show a much greater
degree of unity, they will lose their credibility.

* * *

The divergencies of opinion among Catholics after the
Council has often been described as a conflict between
the vertical and the horizontal, or to put it in simple terms,
should we concentrate more on God or on man? The obvious
answer is that we should do both:'what you have not done to
the least of my brethren, you have not done to me'. Mother
Teresa of Calcutta has shown us a fine way of putting this
into practice. I got to know her personally when she first
visited Sweden in 1974 and I shared the pulpit of the Lutheran
cathedral in Stockholm with her, translating her sermon. She
left her girls school when she discovered how the poor people
around the compound lived and began to devote herself to
the service of the poorest of the poor. I find it encouraging
that she does not write pamphlets and manifestos about her
cause. She and her sisters are too busy for that, taking care
of the urgent need they see, with people dying in the street,
saving newborn babies abandoned among the refuse, helping
lepers, AIDS-patients and the human wrecks in Skid Row,
Los Angeles.

Malcolm Muggeridge made a television film about Mother
Teresa and wrote about it in a book Something Beautiful for
God (which I translated into Swedish). He describes Mother
Teresa "holding a tiny baby girl in her hands; so minute
that her very existence seemed like a miracle. As she holds
this child, she says in a voice, and with an expression of
exaltation most wonderful and moving: 'See! there's life
in her!' Her face is glowing and triumphant; as it might
be the mother of us all glorying in what we all possess —
this life in us, in our world, in the universe, which, however
low it flickers or fiercely it burns, it still a divine flame
which no man dare presume to put out, be his motives
never so humane and enlightened." (p. 29) She is grateful
to Christ "hiding behind the unattractive disguise of the
irritable, the exacting, the unreasonable" patient (p. 75).
How wonderful to serve him without having to expect a
'thank you'.

There is hope for a world which has learnt to appreciate
Mother Teresa and her sisters (who are by no means unique.

Many others are engaged in similar tasks without getting the same publicity for it).

* * *

A final comment before ending this chapter. People used to complain about the youth being so radical. I do not agree. Young people should try new ways and one cannot expect all their ideas to be mature and well thought-out. I am more concerned with the fact that so many of them all too quickly forget their openness and leave their previous enthusiasm behind in order to get ahead and become part and parcel of the security offered by the modern state. The most dramatic example of this comes from the USA. Every spring, the big firms send their scouts to interview students leaving college. After 1968, many radical students had joined the SDS — Students for a Democratic Society. The recruiting officers were told to go for the top figures in the SDS: they were obviously gifted and had shown qualities of leadership and organisation, just the kind of men we need, according to the bosses. It did not take long before many of them had been absorbed by big business and the world of finance and they had become part of the establishment. I do not begrudge them success in life, but I cannot help wondering if this is really the right way to foster the idealism of the youth and enlist their help in building a better world.

Still, I find it much more questionable and deplorable when their enthusiasm is deflected to prop up reactionary movements of neo-nazi or other racial tendencies. Unless we are willing to safeguard the rights of all human beings and let our fight for justice include also those who are not part of our own little group, I fear for the future. I sincerely hope that others won't have to go to war against a new Hitler.

Chapter 18

The Narrow Confines of Human Existence

One day in October, 1958, I went to see Fr Peter Hornung, superior of the Jesuits in Sweden. I was so desperate that I started crying. For eleven long years, I had been studying and preparing myself to work as a Catholic priest in my own country. And now, after only one year in our parish in Stockholm, something had gone wrong and I was unable to carry on. At first, I thought nothing of it. I was just tired and a week or so at the convalescent home of the Sisters of St. Elisabeth outside Stockholm would be all that I needed in order to get back into shape again. But I didn't, nor did two weeks under observation at a hospital get me any further — the doctors were unable to find anything psysically wrong with me. Apart from feeling tired, I suffered from head-aches, dizzy spells, and was oversensitive to light and sound. The neurologist had suggested a possible virus encephalitis or an inflammation of the brain, a diagnosis which did not exist as far as the assistant professor of internal medicine was concerned. So he sent me back home, recommending me to start working again. That was the only cure for it.

It so happened that my father consulted the same professor at this time, and he was asked if I tended to have nerves, complexes etc. My father told him that he had never heard such rubbish and never went back to that doctor again. As for me, I was fetched by car from the hospital, but had to cover my eyes as the traffic made me dizzy, and when I climbed the stairs at the rectory, it got worse and I fell several times. It was after this experience that I went to the superior and started crying.

I was so eager to work, but I could not.

As there were no visible symptoms of my illness, my

156

brethren at first accepted the professor's diagnosis. But one day, I could no longer smoke a cigarette or even drink a glass of beer, and that convinced them: "This is not a case of nerves, the man is ill." A new doctor was called in, a specialist at a hospital for mental disturbances in Uppsala, Ewert Ljungberg. He represented a type of doctor that unfortunately is not very common, combining psychiatry with a good knowledge of the somatic side of medicine. Before starting in on a new case, he always made a thorough general examination to see if the patient did not suffer from some organic disturbance. He then tried to check the internal secretion of hormones, his experience being that a slight imbalance in this respect might be of vital importance. He would even state that all mental disturbances are either caused by such an imbalance in the internal secretion or at least concomitant to it. Consequently, he would try to restore the balance by means of medication before starting the therapy for the so-called nervous illness. A most commendable way of proceeding, to my mind.

In my case, he diagnosed a malfunction of the pituitary gland, probably due to a viral infection of the small brain. He did not have much in the line of medication to suggest — nature would have to heal itself. What I would need was a good rest, which meant doing nothing, and it might take a year or more before I got well again. Not a very cheerful prospect, but I blessed him for letting me be a proper patient, not just an imaginary one.

The kind sisters of St. Elisabeth continued to care for me, now at their nursing home in Stockholm, and I spent almost six months with them. It was a funny kind of a year — I could not read or listen to music, not even play solitaire, and if I tried to walk, the dizziness set in again. There was only one thing I was good at: sleeping, and I would be awake only some eight hours out of the twentyfour.

In the late spring, I was sent to the Black Forest in Germany for rehabilitation and the head of the German Jesuit province (to which I belong) came to visit me. His assistant later told me the the provincial's comments after he left me: "Such a pity. We had finally managed to get a Swedish-born Jesuit, but this man will never again be able to do anything in his life."

Later, I was subjected to pneumoencephalography, which means that they extract 10 cc. of the spinal fluid and inject the same amount of air, which travels to your head and the doctor then takes X-rays of the brain to see if he can find a tumor or other malformation. It was definitely not pleasant, and I would not wish it on my worst enemy (nowadays they use scanning instead). But they found nothing and decided it was "just a virus". The following autumn, after a whole year's break, I could return to the parish and start working again.

It had been a difficult year, and I had learnt to experience within what narrow limits a human has to exist at times. It was by no means the only time I had to spend long periods in a hospital or convalescing: there was St. Clare's hospital in New York, where I was a patient three times. During the long years of study as a Jesuit, I regularly skipped taking proper holidays, spending the summers working in Sweden instead — something I had to pay for later: after ordination, my head refused to absorb any more facts and it took a whole year before I could resume my studies.

Later on, in Uppsala, I had taken on too many different tasks and nature came to my rescue in the form of kidney stones, which had to be removed. By 1980, I had overtaxed myself again, having for years been the only full-time editor of the diocesan paper (22 issues annually), spending most of the "free" periods in Rome working for the Vatican Radio and having extra worries as one of the four members of the diocesan council during a two year period without a bishop. I was completely exhausted and in August 1980 I retired to our summer cottage on the east coast of Gotland, a large island in the middle of the Baltic, expecting to spend a couple of months there, weather permitting. As a matter of fact, I stayed until April, braving the winter in primitive conditions, but the struggle for survival was the right therapy for me. I even got to like my hermit life so much that my friends and relatives started worrying about me. When I finally began working again, I moved to Rome and was able to dedicate myself wholeheartedly to the Scandinavian programme of the Vatican Radio.

These interruptions in normal life were not always easy to accept, but looking back, I realise that they have been valuable to me. St. Clare's hospital gave me my first personal contacts with the Catholic world. When I had to break my theological studies, I was already an ordained priest and thus able to get useful and interesting experience in large parishes, first in Glasgow, visiting people in the slums of Dobie Lane, then in Iserlohn, Germany, this time in a predominantly Lutheran surrounding. Before going to Spain, I spent two months as a chaplain in a US Army hospital in Frankfurt, where my priestly assistance was called upon for every conceivable situation, from patients undergoing gynological examination to the death bed.

I would not have been without that year of hermit life on Gotland for anything. Normally, I am no recluse, but there I experienced another dimension of life and learnt how to function within narrow limits. At the same time, it led me to my present work in Rome, where the scope of work has widened in a way that I could never have dared to dream of.

* * *

Should we then pity mankind, as August Strindberg, the Swedish playwrite and author said? Life is undoubtedly difficult at times. But on the other hand, it is only when we experience our limits that we become aware of the true dimensions of human existence. After all, misfortune is usually not our daily lot. But we are often forced to make choices and realise that opting for one possibility automatically implies excluding many other ones, which might be equally attractive to us, or even more so. The worst kind of reaction to this situation is to clam up and start vegetating, refusing to make any decisions at all.

To wish to do something, and yet be unable to put it into practice, may be disheartening. On the other hand, our very desire is a sign that we are trying to fulfill some of our potentialities. And in the very act of trying, we become aware of the narrow confines of human existence. In this situation, it is important not to get frustrated or dejected but rather let it enrich our lives. An old Greek philosopher said: "I would rather be an unhappy man than a contented pig." Now that is a good motto.

As a priest, one is often confronted with people who have to struggle with life. They come up against physical hurdles like illness, old age or other circumstances beyond their control, what might be called force majeure. The French also use the expression acte de Dieu, apparently having no difficulty in blaming the Lord for it all. Swedes are apt to look upon such an attitude as hiding your head in the sand and they fail to understand how believers can talk about a loving Creator whilst confronted with all this misery.

In my view, it is rather the non-believers who behave like ostriches. I do not close my eyes to all the suffering and misery that exists in the world, but much of it is the result of the fact that we are human beings, which implies having to live within definite limits. This does not mean that I subscribe to the rather perverse view that 'we just get what we deserve'. It is rather a question of trying to see things in another perspective, and grasp the totality, not only the parts. Let yourself be confronted by the wonders of creation, as I did in the Jura mountains, watching the sun rise over the Alps. Or you can do it with the help of modern science. I recently saw a television documentary Design in Nature, describing the regularity and compatibility of the primary building stones without which the structure of organic life would be unthinkable. A Japanese scientist received the Nobel prize in physics (1987) by proving how just a few properties of the DNA molecule can be adapted as a defense against many million kinds of attack against the human cell. With these wonders of nature before our eyes, it is hardly reasonable to look at something like AIDS and say 'how awful everything is!' If someone offers you a plate of excellent soup, you don't have to push it away in disgust just because you happen to find a hair in it.

* * *

We could also look at organic life. It starts pulsing already in the monocell. Textures and organs of the most complicated types are formed in the one egg. The Swedish photographer Lennart Nilsson has produced a remarkable series of pictures which make it possible for us to follow the development from fertilisation to birth. The very process is so complicated that what should really make us wonder is not the rare defects (which are exceptions) but the fact that the end product is usually so perfect.

We might find the polyphony of a Bach fugue or a Mass

by Palestrina complicated, or wish that we had the help of
a score when listening to music by Stravinsky, as he keeps
on changing the rhythm all the time. But it is much more
complicated to try to understand what life is.

A German Jesuit tried to define it and came out with
the following definition (somewhat atypical for a German):
"Life is like music. Who can grasp its ineffable rhythm?"
We have no complete score, with the full list of instruments,
tonalities and tempi, and yet it fills us with its symphony,
letting us surmise the conductor and his cues.

To divine, reflect and partially understand are essential
features of being human. Over and above all the other
wonderful functions, which make up our living being, we
have our intellectual and spiritual capacity, which sometimes
runs riot so that the rest of us cannot keep up with it. We
sort of bubble over and try to break out of our confined
existence. No wonder we occasionally get hurt, especially if
we try to do more than we really can — or should do.

This fact is one of the explanations of the problem of
evil. It would of course be quite wrong to minimise all
the physical suffering that people have to go through. Saint
Francis tried to tackle physical suffering by calling his body
"Brother Ass". But one cannot push it aside by a well-turned
phrase or a quotation from the Bible. I vividly remember
a strong women from southern Sweden, Katarina Stark,
who had become a Catholic and joined the Sisters of St.
Elisabeth. She had crushed several metatarsal bones and
infection had set in, so the doctors warned that they might
have to amputate the foot. When I came to visit her at the
hospital, she held up a warning hand to fend off any wrong
remarks, saying: "Please, Father, no pious words, it is bad
enough as it is."

To confront spiritual or moral Evil is something quite
different. We cannot blame the creator for it — he is the
source of all goodness and the very opposite of evil. We
must realise that part of the responsibility for it falls on our
own shoulders and we have to try to put things right as far
as we can. But we must not sit and brood over our sins and
faults, suggesting that even Our Lord cannot forgive them.

That sin, evil and sheer malice, do exist in this world is
a fact which I feel unable to deny. I cannot get around my

own sins or those committed by others. Here I would like to refer back to my earlier reflections on the horrors of the Nazi regime (though they were by no means the only ones to commit atrocities). Yet the very existence of evil and sin remains a mystery: if God is good and at the same time almighty, one cannot help feeling that he is somehow to be blamed for it. After all, he must have known about it beforehand and could have stopped it, and yet he somehow permits it. The Portuguese try to get around the difficulty with their pious proverb that "God can write straight on crooked lines", which sounds nice.

Perhaps there are limits even for the Almighty. If he wants to create beings with free will, he has to reckon with the possibility that they are going to use it the wrong way. Otherwise, they would be just robots, or so overpowered by his light that they would not be able to see any alternatives.

* * *

Now even if much of what we call the problem of evil is the result of human limitations, it certainly does not explain everything. It becomes most acute when physical and moral evil co-exist. It is quite astounding to find within what narrow and inhuman limits a human being can exist — read some of the accounts of what people managed to survive in Himmler's concentration camps.

For a Christian, there is one example which is even more striking. "The Word was made flesh", God became man and showed that within the narrow limits of human existence, there was room for the Divine to act. And just look at his limits: his life finished at the age of only 33, and on the cross. It certainly looked like a complete failure.

But maybe Our Lord suggests an answer to our questions. He was jeered and they said to him: "If you are indeed the Son of God, why do you not step down from the cross?" He could have, but he did not want to do so. The cross has become a sign of victory, to help us understand how far God is willing to go to show his love for us and to elicit our return of love. Here the veil surrounding the mystery of our salvation is lifted.

* * *

I recently read an article on care of terminal cases and it had been given a good heading: "Death is not a failure."

The only certain thing in our uncertain life is that we shall once die. But St. Paul cries out, triumphantly (I Cor 15.55). "Death, where is thy victory, where is thy sting?" He does it, fully convinced that Christ is truly risen and that we shall all share in the life that he came to give us, and a full and an overflowing measure of it. If I were not convinced of this, I would long ago have given up being a priest and a Jesuit.

I have had the privilege to sit at many deathbeds and am fully aware of the fact that it is difficult when you reach the borders of this life. But at the same time, I do not find it an empty phrase when you talk about the dying person "going home". When you watch their last gaze, it seems that they have already had a glimpse of eternity. It is not just something reserved for those officially proclaimed saints.

I consider it demeaning if you try to hide away the dying person. One should not experiment with them to try to keep them alive a bit longer, and definitely not keep them sedated and then let them die alone in cubby-hole. They need help and support at this very important moment. I was once a patient in a general ward in Stockholm when an old man in the next bed had a heart attack. He cried out softly but was unable to call for the nurse. I got up and asked him: "Is there anything I can do for you?" And he answered: "Please hold my hand." That made him feel better.

Mother Teresa and her sisters get out in to the streets of Calcutta and look for human beings who have been left to die by themselves. They take them to their house for the dying. There are people who regret that the sisters waste time on such hopeless cases instead of helping the living. Mother Teresa smiles at such remarks and says: "Should they not experience human love and kindness, at least for a few hours or days?" It is almost as if she were saying: "How could they recognise God, who is love, if they have never met any one willing to show them love on this earth?"

Among my favourite prayers is the one that the priest recites at a deathbed. The Church has already anointed the dying person with the sacrament of the sick to help her to end this life and enter eternity.

She then recommends the dying person to the Lord. It is almost as if the Church avails herself of all the authority she has received and sends the soul on her way:

Profisciscere anima christiana...go forth you Christian soul out of this world,

in the name of God, the almighty Father, who has created you,

in the name of Jesus Christ, the Son of the living God, who has suffered for you,

in the name of the Holy Spirit, who has been poured out over you,

in the name of the angels and the archangels, of the principalities and the powers, in the name of cherubim and serafim, in the name of the patriarchs and the prophets...

It is almost as if you could hear the song of praise of the angels. Cardinal Newman has written a wonderful poem about this called The Dream of Gerontius. Gerontius is dying and the priest and Gerontius' friends are praying for him. We follow his struggle until he commends his soul to the Lord. Now the priest intones the prayer Profisciscere over him and the choir takes up the words "Go forth". Elgar has set music to it in his oratory, and it sounds like a triumphal march. And what better occasion can we find for Pomp and Circumstance?

Life is like music. Personally, I hope that eternal life is going to burst forth in an enticing sound, which carries us beyond time and space into the everpresent NOW.

Chapter 19

Rome and the Vatican Radio

It was not yet time for the final trumpets but more than one of my friends were willing to blow their horn for joy on learning that I was leaving my hermitage on the island of Gotland. Some of them had made their own diagnose of what was wrong with me and had feared that I would never get over it. Apparently it was difficult for them to accept the easy answer that I was worn out and had to lie fallow for a while before being able to resume an active life.

I now had to decide what kind of job I would be able and willing to assume. I did not want to return to the diocesan magazine, having spent too many and laborious years with it. I had reached the age of 59 and they say that is your last chance in life to change jobs.

What about getting into radio properly? I had had a soft spot for it ever since we had acquired a simple crystal receiver in the early 1930's. Soon afterwards, a technical student boarding with us had built a more advanced receiver and I started listening to shortwave broadcasts. I decided to become a licenced amateur operator and when registering for military service I asked to be assigned to the Signal Corps. On my continental trip during the summer of 1939, I had brought along a list of all the European radio amateurs and looked up several of them. But the war intervened and, as I have described in earlier chapters, I did not serve with the Swedish Army nor in a Signal Corps. During my time as a priest in Uppsala, I had met some local amateurs and finally got my own licence with the call sign SM5BOE. If I were to start telling about the satisfaction and enjoyment I have had of that hobby, I would have to write another book.

When I came back home to Sweden in 1957, having finished my training as a Jesuit, I was asked to produce material
for the Swedish programmes of the Vatican Radio which had
been initiated a couple of years earlier. It only involved
preparing manuscripts for two 15 min. programmes per
month which were then sent to a speaker in Rome. Later on,
the Scandinavian transmissions were extended and recording
equipment installed in a makeshift studio in the wardrobe of
my flat in Uppsala. It was not until 1965 that I travelled to
Rome for the first time in order to report on the closing
session of the Second Vatican Council. It was quite an
experience to meet the worldwide church in such a concrete
way with some 3 000 bishops from almost every country
on the face of the earth assembled in St. Peter's basilica.
During breaks one had to elbow one's way through a whole
crowd of prelates. During the intervals they would meet for
a cup of coffee in one of the bars installed in the church
and chat almost like students. Archbishop Bruno Heim (then
papal representative in Scandinavia, later nuntio in London)
commented that the council was a good thing for the bishops.
For the first time they had the sobering experience of being
just one of a huge group. Unfortunately, not every one
remembered the lesson when they returned home.

From now on I went to Rome three times a year and
became more familiar with both the Vatican Radio and
the workings of the central administration of the Catholic
Church. In 1968 I got my first permanent collaborator,
Ingrid Amici, a student from Uppsala who had married
an orthopedic surgeon in Rome, and from then on she
was the mainstay of the programme. In those days, it was
considered a privilege to work for the Vatican and the pay
was negligible. A Swedish weekly interviewing Ingrid used
the following heading: The Voice of the Holy Spirit, Paid
with Food Coupons. The last bit referred to the permission
to buy food at the tax free store inside the Vatican and it
was probably worth more than the cash she was paid. I
am glad to say that the demands for social justice have
resulted in more equitable renumerations since then and
Vatican collaborators receive not only reasonable salaries
but have a pension scheme and health insurance. This is
of course reflected in the yearly budget and explains why

the Vatican is so much in the red these days. More than half of the current expenses goes to salaries and pensions.

During the following years we were able to enlarge the Scandinavian service further. Seeing that many reports on our transmissions came from Finland, I realised the need to start a programme in Finnish. I was lucky to find a Finnish nun working in Rome, sister Benedicta Idefeldt. She had spent most of her religious life working in Germany and Brasil and was afraid that she had forgotten her mother tongue. But she soon picked it up anew and rediscovered her roots visisting her home country regularly (she has written an autobiography From Viborg to the Vatican, which became a bestseller in Finland). The response to our Finnish programmes has been most satisfactory and they account for 40% of the letters we receive from the Scandinavian region.

Leaving Gotland I was able to start working fulltime for the Vatican Radio, a decision that I have not regretted in any way. I found it very satisfying finally to be able to do the job properly. Working in Rome is very stimulating. The various language sections of the Vatican Radio are given a good deal of freedom when it comes to shaping their programs. It so happens that there is no one in the Vatican administration who understands our northern languages, which gives me a further freedom but I try not to take undue advantage of it. Loyalty to the Church and the Pope place their demands on us, but we have a way of expressing ourself which is adapted to our audience. The vast majority of them are what I call normal Scandinavians, that is members of the Lutheran church who do not know too much about their own religion and nothing about the Catholic church.

The contents of our programmes reflect this fact. There are short quotes from the Pope's speeches and official statements, news about the Catholic world, including Scandinavia, comments on debates current in Scandinavian media. We give a great deal of publicity to the papal journeys, including the background information, seeing that the media in the northern countries hardly mention his trips. We receive some 1,000 letters yearly with comments and can judge both who our listeners are, the extent to which they were able to grasp what we were talking about and what they would like to hear. The listeners can be divided into three categories: the youngsters who start out listening to shortwave broadcasts, so-called DX-ers, those who restart listening at the age of around 35, having settled down and founded a family, and finally a number of old age pensioners, who like to listen to broadcasts in their own language.

When I arrived in Rome in 1981 there was a crisis in the English-speaking programme and for a while, I was asked to be responsible for it. That is probably the reason why I was given the opportunity to participate in some papal journeys. The first one was in May/June 1982 when I was in Edinburgh reporting on the Scottish part of the papal visit. I had been to the city before and was at first confirmed in my judgement that it is cool, snooty and Calvinistic. But when the Pope arrived, they all fell for him. The moderator of the Presbyterian church and his elders (together with their wives) stood in line to greet him, right under the huge statue of John Knox, the Calvinist reformer, who had previously been a Catholic priest. What would his comment have been?

It was a very hot June that year, most unusual for Scotland. Due to lack of space, there was no room for us in the archbishop's house and they had installed the Vatican Radio studio in the cardinal's pottery, where he grew his tomatoes. It was sweltering inside and the modern transistorised equipment did not like it; they had to change the telex apparatus several times.

Later that year I was sent to Spain to cover another papal trip. I first stayed in Zaragossa and then went on to Santiago de Compostella, a place which I remember especially for the constant rain we had and the cool reception given us at the archbishop's palace.

Having started daily programmes for Scandinavia I thought that by now I had had my share of papal trips. To my surprise and pleasure I was asked to go to Papua New Guinea to cover the papal visit there in May 1984. I had never been to South East Asia before. I was deeply impressed with the native population. They seemed to be serene and to have a profound spiritual dimension. This I found surprising as the vast majority of them have been living in mountainous regions which are so isolated that there are over 700 different languages (not dialects) on the island. Until a short time ago, much of the island was a white spot on the map and during World War II, the Japanese considered the mountain regions of the country to be a natural barrier which neither needed nor could be fortified. The life style of the Papuans has been unchanged for many centuries and it is a wonder that they now manage to leave what was more or less the Stone Age and enter the modern world without suffering too much of a cultural shock. A successful Papuan has written an autobiography aptly entitled: 12,000 Years in a Lifetime.

On my way back to Europe I spent a week in Manila, a city with as many inhabitants as the whole of Sweden. I really fell for the charming Philippine people and have been following the progress of their nation ever since (I was there towards the end of the Marcos period). But when I got back to Rome, I felt that it was nice to be once again in a city without too many cars, relatively few traffic problems and negligible fumes. It all depends on your standard of comparison.

Two years later I was on my first 'real' papal trip, that is travelling in the papal plane together with members of the international press corps covering the entire journey. During a couple of hectic weeks in November 1986, we visited Dacca, Singapore, the Fiji Islands, New Zealand, Australian and the Seychelles. It was anything but a tourist trip. I don't think that I have ever slept as little, worked as hard and perspired as much as I did that fortnight. Pope John Paul II has a gift for languages but his vocabulary does not seem to include the expression "jet lag". People ask how he manages to survive the trips. Admittedly he has to bear a very heavy burden but it is a fact that the journalists are pushed even more. They have to be out at the airport long before the Pope arrives and in the evening, they spend long hours working in the pressroom before snatching a few hours of sleep in the hotel room. We had three stops in New Zealand and then visited nine cities and all the states in Australia, which is a not only a country but a continent. One day we started in Melbourne in the southwest, travelled to Darwin in the northernmost part of the country, where an outdoor mass was celebrated under a sweltering tropical sun. About midday, we proceeded to Alice Springs in the centre of Australia for a meeting with the aboriginals (who seemed to have fared much more badly

than the Papuans). Before the last lap of the day, we had
an extra hour in the plane, waiting for a violent storm to
subside. Late in the evening we arrived in Adelaide in the
southern part of the continent where there was a torch light
procession through the city. The journalists then gathered in
the pressroom, eating sandwiches and drinking beer while
sending off our dispatches or taping our reports. I later
checked the mileage we had covered that day. It equalled
the distance between Stockholm and Nairobi in Kenya, and
we had had quite a programme during the day. It was an
interesting and exciting experience, but you felt the need of
a break after it.

*   *   *

People often ask me: "Do you meet the Holy Father often."
I used to answer that I see him often at a distance, and
every now and again close up when joining a Swedish
group attending a papal audience. After a while, he seemed
to recognize me but he did not recall who I was.

However, in June 1989, the Pope visited all the Scandinavian or northern countries, Norway, Iceland, Finland, Denmark and Sweden. The Scandinavian section of the Vatican
Radio was fully engaged in preparing this journey. Not as
far as plans, programme and speeches were concerned, but
all the texts in Scandinavian languages had to be checked by
our people, as no one else in the Vatican understood them.
We also became a focal point for the journalists from Scandinavia who wanted to learn something about the Vatican,
and they kept on coming. With the help of the Swedish
ambassador to the Holy See and the Papal Commission for
Social Communication, we arranged a study week in Rome
and the Vatican for journalists from our countries and all
of 68 of them turned up.

Our highest priority of course was to be at the disposition of the Holy Father, who always tries to learn something of the languages of the region he visits. That meant
four Scandinavian languages, Swedish, Danish, Norwegian
and Icelandic plus Finnish, which is entirely different. It
does not belong to the Indoeuropean family of languages
but has origins from south of the Ural mountains and is
similar to Hungarian, Estonian and the Lapp languages.
It is impossible to learn it in a short time, but it has one

advantage: the stress is always on the first syllable and everything is pronounced as it is written, though the words may be long. The Scandinavian languages, on the other hand, show great similarity in writing but are more tricky as the pronounciation and melody varies considerably.

Members of the Scandinavian section were called on to assist the Holy Father in his language studies. It meant going through texts, helping with the pronounciation and the interpretation of what was written. We also had to translate further texts as the Holy Father wanted more than had been sent from Scandinavia. Our preparations were somewhat hindered by the fact that another papal trip to Africa intervened, with more native languages to be studied. But Pope John Paul II is not only ambitious but very gifted when it comes to languages. I tried to warn him about the difficulty in remembering the melody of the various languages, especially during a short and quick trip through the Scandinavian countries. But he was undaunted and turned out to learn much more than anyone could have imagined. I have never had a pupil who was so highly motiviated and who managed to learn so much in a such short time. Members of our section went to the papal palace for at least two live sessions each with the Holy Father. We also made casettes with all the speeches and the liturgy, and he kept on listening to them, making remarkable progress.

I was included among the international journalists on the Scandinavian trip and had the opportunity to cross over to the papal party whenever needed. It was a great experience for me as a Swede. I was surprised how well it all worked out. Only some 15 or 20 years ago, it would have been quite unthinkable to invite the Pope to Scandinavia. Except for some minor demonstrations by a few Lutheran bishops in Norway and Denmark, the reception was warm amd friendly. In Sweden, the Lutheran archbishop of Uppsala and the bishop of Stockholm, as well as the moderator of the congregationalists, attached themselves to the line of communicants at the Pope's mass. They did not receive communion but asked the Pope to bless them. Such an action would have caused a major outcry some years ago; now it seemed quite natural. The next day, in Uppsala, started with an ecumenical service and was followed by a reception in the archbishop's residence with representatives of practically every church and religious community in Sweden. It turned into a joyful family affair where the Holy Father could feel at home, and it seemed as if almost all of them looked at him as a pater familias and a friend.

That is the thing about John Paul II. He is very conscious of the fact that he is the Pope. At the same time, he steps out of the role to become a fellow human being who is equally conscious about the people around him, what they need and what they care about. Looking at it, from my own point of view, the Scandinavian papal visit meant that I had the privilege to get to know both pope John Paul II and Karol Wojtyla, a person I had not met before. Somewhat presumiously I venture to look upon him as my friend, though being fully aware that we probably will not meet again in the same way, person to person.

* * *

The most dramatic incidence with the Pope was of course on May 13, 1981, when an attempt was made on his life during the general audience in St. Peter's square. I happened to be on the second floor of the broadcasting house when I saw the head of programmes come running along the corridor; not his usual style. He was immediately followed by the director general, Fr. Tucci, running at full pace and I realised that something extraordinary was going on. Soon the sound of sirens from a large number of police cars filled the air. All the current programmes of the Vatican Radio were immediately cancelled and Fr. Tucci took over. In several languages, and over all our transmittors simultaneously, he gave out whatever information we could obtain. For a while, the Vatican Radio became the primary source of information for all the news agencies.

A few days later, the Holy Father was able to say a few words over the Radio from his hospital bed. He began by praying for the two ladies who had been injured together with him and then proceeded to pray "for this brother of mine" who was responsible for the attempt on his life. Several years later, in 1987, Ali Agca's mother came to Rome to visit her son. She asked to meet the Pope in order to beg his pardon for what her son had done. The Pope reassured her that he had forgiven Ali a long time ago and had told him so personally when visiting him in the prison. The Pope then gave Ali's mother his blessing, and she knelt down towards the East and prayed to Allah for the Holy Father.

* * *

I have now become somewhat of a Roman, even if I retain a room in Uppsala and spend part of the year there. In 1986, I became a senior citizen, but it has not changed my way of life. I consider myself lucky to be able to continue working and to devote myself to something that gives me great satisfaction. Our listeners keep on writing to us and their comments are usually favourable. Their main objection seems to be that we have only 19 minutes daily at our disposal, but there are 50 programmes in over 40 languages competing for transmission time at the Vatican Radio.

I find it stimulating to work in such international surroundings and I live in a community of some 60 Jesuits from 28 countries. Every road leads to Rome, they say, and it is true: as I walk from our house to the office, along the Via della Conciliazione, the avenue between St. Peter's basilica and the Tiber, I see people from all over the world and hear a multitude of languages.

I am not an expert on Roman art, being something of an anti-tourist. I like art, but not museums. If I can look at a few pictures at a time, I appreciate them, but when they offer me hundreds and thousands of them, a psychological block sets in. I prefer to walk around the old part of the city, watching people. Thanks to the climate, so much of the life of the Romans takes place in the streets and I rate their quality of life high. At home in Sweden, rationalisation is the catch word and you do not get many personal contacts in your daily life, outside the people you work with. Rome is different. Even in the centre of town, shops, restaurants and most of the service industry are on a family basis. There is the husband and wife, a cousin or inlaw, who will greet you as an old friend the second time you enter their shop. The street leading up from behind our radio house to the Vatican is filled with such small establishments. Many shopkeepers stand in the doorway, ready to chat, and the street is like a small village where almost everbody greets you.

No wonder I feel at home in Rome.

Chapter 20

Looking Back — An Evaluation

As I come to the end of my autobiography, there is a question which almost poses itself: "Now, what was it really like? After all these years as a priest and a Jesuit, am I satisfied, or have I regretted my choice?"

Edith Piaf used to sing a song with the title Rien, je ne regrette rien — no, I don't regret anything at all. She lived a rather different kind of life from mine, but I would like to concur with the main theme. Obviously I have made my mistakes and committed sins, but I hope that I have also repented. Even mistakes can have a salutary effect, though you have to be careful not to turn them into virtues, just because they taught you a useful lesson.

One thing I have never regretted, not for one moment, is having become a Catholic. On the contrary, it has enriched my life in a way that probably nothing else could have done. Nor do I at all regret having entered the Society of Jesus, which is the official name of my religious order. To many, and not only Swedish Protestants, the word Jesuit sounds almost sinister, but I have got to know the order from the inside. I won't say that it is always perfect and beyond criticism, but my relation to it has mainly been positive. It is a family to which I belong and of which I am a member. A German Jesuit, Fr. Ernst Bömminghaus, once said to his young brethren: "Remember, in religious life, you share your life as brothers and sisters in Christ with persons with whom you probably would have had nothing to do in normal life."

That is an important reminder, as Jesuits are not all of one cut. You cannot expect a natural mutual sympathy to develop automatically between all the members of a religious order. In a marriage, you choose your partner for life, whereas in religious life, we did not choose the brethren, but chose the order as a way to serve God and Christ. In other words, it is Him we seek, not each other. We may have different backgrounds, and often quite different lines of interest in life, yet we are all convinced that the Lord wants us to serve Him in the Society of Jesus. Fortunately, there is a fair amount of leeway in the Society, otherwise it would be difficult for us to fit in together and make our contribution in our own individual way and yet in common.

Now if I am to be quite sincere — something I have aimed at in my narrative — I must admit that I felt more at home in the English Jesuit province than in the German one, to which I belong. But all the same, I do not regret my choice. I joined a German province because they have been sending Jesuits to Sweden since 1879, and I did want to work as a priest in my own country. Looking back, I also realise that, though I felt very much at home with my English friends, the scope of their activities was primarily confined to their schools, especially boarding schools like Stonyhurst and Beaumont. Other fields, such as social action, did not rank high among their priorities. I do not think it unfair to say that the English Jesuit province was not very dynamic, at least not in my days.

The German province might have its shortcomings and its flaws, but they also had a wider perspective (though at times they stress the importance of the intellectual sphere a bit too much for my taste). It happens that I let go of the word 'German' with a sigh, but I have no reason to believe that life would have been completely serene if I had been surrounded only by Swedish brethren. Admittedly, it was not always easy to be the only one and only 'native' Swede in a small community of 'foreigners', who had a common Germanic cultural background. But on the other hand, it was probably not always easy for them to have me in their midst, as I can be both argumentative and provocative, when so inclined.

* * *

I can imagine many a reader asking: How on earth could anyone become a Jesuit and take vows of poverty, obedience and chastity. That is surely something you must have regretted — or ignored, when you found it too inconvenient.

In reply I wish to return to the words of Edith Piaf: I regret nothing. That does not mean that everything has been easy, or perfect. Let me start with the vow of poverty. It was strictly observed when I joined the Society of Jesus in 1946 and our lifestyle was much restricted by it, but that did not bother me, it was part of the life I had chosen. Later on, my experience has been that it is to a certain extent up to the individual how he interprets and fulfills the vow. The restrictions connected with it applies primarily to the individual — as a community, there is always some one who sees to it that we have a roof over our head, enough to eat and subsist, sometimes even with comfort. In the words of the Gospel, we may have given up everything, but at the same time, we are not subject to the cares and worries about daily existence that most people around us have.

The vow of obedience might seem even desirable to the young Jesuit — entering religious life, you want to place yourself at the full disposal of the Lord, and what is more reasonable than to leave all the vital decisions to your superior, representing the will of God for you. As time passes, however, and you get more entrenched in special spheres of activities, it becomes more difficult to have the same confidence in your superior, especially when his views do not coincide with your own on important matters. However, you can't have your cake and eat it. What is the point of taking a vow of obedience if the superior always follows your opinions? It is only when you get a strict, or even awkward, superior that you have to start living up to the vow properly, realising what it means to put your trust in the Lord in that rather special way.

By this I do not want to imply that Jesuits often have to suffer under difficult superiors; I rather imagine that, among us too, it is more common to complain about the lack of good leaders, capable of planning and willing to take full responsibility for the coordination and implementation of the same. Much has been written about the blind obedience expected of a Jesuit, who should 'let himself be guided as docilely as a corpse carried on a litter'. The phrase is found in our constitutions, but it is in fact a quote from St. Francis.

Ignatius did indeed want his followers to be obedient, but he stressed that it should be an intelligent form of obedience, where you are supposed to present your arguments to the superior and to interpret the directives you get in a rational way. There is even a classical example of the superior who was several times ordered by Ignatius himself to do things in a certain way and yet did them his way, telling Ignatius why. In the end, he was commended for the way he had acted, seeing that he knew the local conditions better.

On one point, however, Ignatius is most emphatic: if a Jesuit finds that executing the command he has received from the superior should involve committing a sin, even a minor one, he must refuse. The end does not justify the means.

There remains the vow of chastity. Maybe there is a reader eagerly awaiting interesting revelations. In that case, I must disappoint him, the main reason being that I do not have much to offer in that line.

Let me first point out that there is a certain difference between celibacy and the vow of chastity. Celibacy is a disciplinary rule in the Latin church, which means that a candidate for the priesthood — before ordination — has to make a solemn promise to his bishop to remain unmarried and to lead a life of continence. Under certain circumstances, a dispensation from it be can be obtained, and celibacy has indeed not always been prescribed, or fully adhered to, in the history of the Church. It is, however, not to be looked upon solely as a disciplinary measure, but rather as a sacrifice asked of the prospective priest and a way to encourage him to follow the way of Christ.

Members of religious orders freely choose to take a vow of chastity, whether they will be ordained or not. They find their motivation in the words of Christ talking to the disciples about the indissolubility of marriage. The disciples protested (Mt 19.10) saying that in that case, it would be better not to marry at all. Christ then suggested the possibility of renouncing marriage and talked of chastity as a gift, though not for all, and he added: "There are eunuchs born that way from their mother's womb, there are eunuchs made so by men and there are eunuchs who have made themselves that way for the sake of the kingdom of heaven. Let anyone accept this who can." (Mt.19.12 — Jerusalem Bible).

Let me stress that I have never looked upon myself as some kind of a gelding — or even less as "sexless", which is the curious way our latest Swedish version of the New Testament has put it. It should be clear to readers of previous chapters that I am not devoid of feelings for the opposite sex; on the other hand, as I have previously mentioned, our early romantic attachments were kept within much stricter limits than seems to be the case nowadays. Without trying to withold things from my reader, I fail to see that an inventory of my sexual experience before my becoming a Jesuit could be of much interest to anyone. Be it sufficient to say that when I became a Catholic at the age of 21, I looked upon it as a obligation not to indulge in promiscuity. It was not always easy, especially not during my period as a soldier, when the initiative often came from the other side (though a girl did tell me once: "If you hadn't been such a convinced Catholic, you would probably have been quite a Don Juan"). When I entered the Jesuit order, I soon had the opportunity of taking my first, temporary vows, including that of chastity, and this I did because I felt called to it, and afterwards I have kept to it. I do not say this to brag, but only to state the simple truth.

In spite of this, I wish to repeat that I no means look upon myself as a gelding, and I do not think that is the way I appear to people, either. I am by no means devoid of feelings — by nature I am rather of the choleric type. When I was a small boy, I got my weekly allowance only if I chopped and delivered enough wood at our weekend cottage, and it suited me fine, because at times I got rather worked up and could get rid of my aggression with the help of an axe and a chopping block. You may remember from an earlier chapter how my old Jesuit teacher of Latin taught us not to try to get rid of our passions, but rather use them as driving forces to reach our goals in life. That was an important lesson. We must not just let loose all the forces that we find within ourselves and permit them to drag us their way. It is vitally important to learn to keep them in rein and steer them, using their power to take you in the direction you want to develop as a person.

If anyone suggests that I made a great sacrifice by promising chastity, I agree, though perhaps for different reasons. I would gladly have married, and there were two women with whom I have been truly in love: Emmele in Ecuador and Elena in New York. To share a married life with either of them seemed a very desirable future. But I came up against a difficulty: I could not imagine any civil profession, which would satisfy me fully. To be a religious and a priest was the only really meaningful thing to me, and that meant having to renounce the possibility of marrying.

It was definitely a sacrifice. It was not only a question of having to give up some one who was close to me, but it also meant renouncing the joy and intimacy of family life, which does not only mean the union of man and wife but also includes the children, which I hope that the good Lord would have given us. That, to my mind, is the real sacrifice of chastity, not the question of continence. Frankly, I do not think being chaste is all that difficult, if you have the right motivation for it and the conviction that the sacrifice is worth it. Even some one like Suzanne Brøgger, a Danish writer famous for her candid revelations, has lately said that sexuality resides more in the brain than in the loins. In other words, motivation is the springing point, not the libido. Maybe this is something for our present generation to ponder on after all the experimentation in other directions.

Still, I personally feel that before making a vow or promise of chastity, one should preferably know what it means to be in love. It is a fundamental dimension of human life, and if you have had no experience of it, there is likely to be something lacking in your personal development, and furthermore, you do not really understand what it is that you are renouncing. This does not necessarily have to include sexual initiation: take for instance the balcony scene in Shakespeare's Romeo and Juliet, or Paul Geraldy's Toi et Moi. The latter is the story of a couple, who obviously have an improper relationship, and yet this exquisite poetry does not primarily deal with sex, but describes love between two individuals.

* * *

Looking back, my need is to count my blessings, not the possible sum total of any sacrifices. I feel a bit like the man who was asked why he believed in God, and he answered: "I have to have some one to say 'Thank you' to!" I was given a good start in my youth, in spite of certain shadows. I have lived a full and eventful life, which opened up many new angles for me, and, I hope, also taught me some valuable lessons. It has not exactly been a bed of roses, but there were very few instances when I wanted to be someone else, or be somewhere else. Surely, that is a sign of having lived a privileged life.

There are so many to whom I should turn in order to show my gratitude for all this. But most of all, I wish to thank the good Lord, who led me along these unexpected paths and who has enriched my life so much. So let my memoirs be a sign of this gratitude, and if they help to give hope and courage to any of my readers, I shall feel doubly rewarded.